Real World Proven
Best Business Practices

Rangitawa
PUBLISHING

Real World Proven
Best Business Practices

Bridging the Gap Between Academic Teachings and Real World Business Success

Peter Alexander

Real World Proven Best Business Practices-Bridging the Gap Between Academic Teachings and Real World Business Success.

Published by Rangitawa Publishing, Feilding, New Zealand. 2016.

Logo design Matt Alexander.

ISBN 978-0-9941382-3-1

www.rangitawapublishing.com
rangitawa@xtra.co.nz

www.realworldconsulting.kiwi

Contents

Real World
Consulting
PROVEN BEST PRACTICES FOR
SURVIVING AND THRIVING IN BUSINESS

The Gap Between Academic Teachings and the Real World Business Environment

Peter Alexander is a Kiwi (New Zealand citizen) who graduated from Massey University (Palmerston North, New Zealand) in 1990 with a Bachelor of Business Studies Degree (Marketing major).

Peter's passion for learning, and identifying where improvements to processes/ practices/ methodology can be made, has led him on a successful commercial career path to date - spanning a diverse range of industries and businesses since graduating.

Through fulfilling Chief Executive Officer, General Manager and other similar roles for the majority of his working life to date, Peter has developed considerable knowledge, skills and experience in the commercial world; and most importantly has come to deeply understand what the Critical Success Factors (CSF's) are that are common to most businesses irrespective of their scale, customer value proposition (product/ service offering) or industry association...factors which many businesses seemingly simply don't understand or do understand yet don't assign enough importance or value to when setting strategic or operational plans.

Given his natural bent towards providing vision, direction and guidance to others, in 2016 Peter pursued a role as a Business Advisor within the Regional Business Partner programme which operates across New Zealand. This central government funded and coordinated programme focuses on helping Kiwi businesses to develop and grow, involving appointed Business Advisors objectively determining the capability development needs of businesses and how these gaps/ needs could best be resolved. Peter operated in this advisory capacity in the Hawke's Bay region, and was exposed to a wide range of businesses in terms of product/ service, delivery focus, scale of operation, industry type, and stage of commercial evolution and maturity.

Peter is concerned about the apparent gap in "real world commercial understanding" that seems to exist in the case of many business owners, between acquired academic knowledge and the practical skills/ knowledge/ capability that need to be an inherent part of a business owner's DNA if their business is to survive and thrive.

Others – such as Dan Browne (President of the Young Professionals, Hawke's Bay) – who are in roles which provide them with first-hand insight into the difficulties facing newly tertiary qualified and established business people alike can also see this gap, and are concerned that graduates are arguably not being equipped well enough during their tertiary studies to be able to convince employers that they can indeed "hit the ground running" adding value to employers' businesses soon after being appointed.

"There is a massive gap between employer expectations and what young people are trained to be. The base skills employers are wanting and are looking for aren't actually being trained into these kids." [reference: editorial provided by Dan Browne, published in the 'Hawke's Bay Today' newspaper on 21st November, 2014].

Through this book and the management roles that Peter continues to apply himself to, he hopes to make a positive difference to the survival and success rate of businesses – most particularly those which are of a SME (Small Medium Enterprise) scale - in New Zealand and in other parts of the world.

PREFACE

I have a sincere passion for guiding/ leading people to win and to be the best at what they do, which is one of the two underlying motivations that has led me to write this book. The second prompt for me committing to write this book is the despair I feel when I hear/ read about yet another Kiwi business having been placed in receivership, or the failure rate of Kiwi businesses being pretty much what it was when I was completing my Bachelor Degree (i.e. depending on what source is relied upon for this dim insight, it is estimated that overall between 25 - 50 % of Kiwi businesses fail within 5 - 10 years from starting-up), or the high employee turnover rates which characterize some Kiwi businesses.

Another concerned Kiwi echoes this perception of the tragedy which is the failure rate of particularly SME scale businesses in New Zealand with this article:

http://www.stuff.co.nz/business/smallbusiness/79068 92/Where-is-New-Zealand-Inc-going-wrong

Excerpts from this article...

"The death rate of small to medium businesses in New Zealand is a national tragedy, reckons Peter Sun of Waikato University."

"Among SMEs born between 2001 and 2009, of those employing zero people - mum and dad operations - 69 per cent failed; of those employing 1-5 people, 51 per cent failed; and of those employing 6-9 and 10-19, 45 per cent had failed by 2009."

"... in 2009 there were also more deaths than births of businesses, according to 2010 statistics from the former Economic Development Ministry."

During my time to date in senior management roles (working in companies that ranged from $3.5m sales turnover p.a. to around $500m sales turnover p.a.) I observed a close connection and correlation between the success of a business and the extent to which a business evolves by focusing on its <u>Critical Success Factors</u>; and concluded that the more committed a business is to shaping and driving its strategic direction and operational delivery focusing on its Critical Success Factors, the more quickly the given business will evolve and attain its operational and strategic objectives, and the greater will be its overall success (commercial and cultural).

Conversely, I also observed that the less inclined a business is to base its evolutionary course and commercial future on implementing action which is strongly focused on its Critical Success Factors, the higher the probability that the given business will fail to realize its aspirations (commercial and cultural).

I then took this deliberation one stage further, and started to look at why the latter category of business owners tend to (often at their peril) shun or ignore the notion of channelling available resources into those areas/activities of their business which represent Critical Success Factors; and came to realize that in many cases such business owners simply do not acquire a suitable depth of concrete practical commercial knowledge to know what Critical Success Factors must be present in a business in order for it to survive and thrive.

I concluded that a major reason why so many small to medium sized businesses fail during the first 1 – 2 years of them starting-up is due to the owners of these businesses failing to acquire the necessary concrete practical commercial knowledge and skills to enable them – irrespective of whether the owner(s) had the good fortune of undertaking tertiary business studies or not - to plan and operate with a strong focus on those factors which are critical to their commercial survival and success.

From my own experience of completing a university degree, in my opinion a sizeable chunk of commercial knowledge that is available via academia can sometimes tend to be highly theoretical in nature, and therefore does not readily lend itself to being applied in a practical way in the real business world, to quickly generate commercial value for the business that the graduating student enters.

I have prepared this book as an endeavour to help equip particularly graduating commerce students and new-to-business business people/ owners in New Zealand and around the world with a practical understanding of business practices that are <u>proven</u> to help business owners and managers firstly survive and then thrive in the real world of business.

Luck is not responsible for most commercial success – nor is success due to any magic tricks or secret formula. Rather, success in business mostly comes from individuals channelling their time, effort, energies and skills into activities that are responsible for producing success (i.e. the Critical Success Factors of the given business).

1.0 Introduction: The Gap Between Academia and the Real Business World

It is sometimes reported in the media that the gap between the knowledge and skills that graduating tertiary students have, compared to the expectations that employers have of these people is significant. I am aware that some employers avoid employing newly graduated students due to their belief that new graduates are entering the real business world without a sufficient practical knowledge base which will enable them to add value to employers' businesses within a short space of time of them entering the given business.

I think there is most certainly a well-deserved place for universities and similar tertiary education providers to help prepare interested commerce students for life in the business world, yet I also consider and advocate that greater emphasis could be placed on providing commerce students with a wider and deeper range of practical knowledge and skills for them to apply as soon as they enter their first role in the real world of business – irrespective of whether that role is one of a business owner or an employee at whatever level.

To be clear, I have not written this book to either scrutinize or criticize the value of tertiary education organizations in helping people to become productive, useful and valuable contributors in the workforce. Anyone interpreting the messages within this book in this way is in fact misinterpreting the purpose and intention of this book.

Rather, I intend this book to serve as a helpful (supplementary) bridge between commercial knowledge gained via academia and the real world of business. My sincere hope is that this book will in some way help business owners avoid common pitfalls that cause many businesses to fail, and assist businesses to evolve more positively and at a faster rate in order to become the best that they can be in their respective industries...and in doing so perhaps even become commendable international players.

18

This book is about keeping the message "short and sweet", using "concrete, down-to-earth" language - so that the information within can be quickly understood, digested and applied by business owners/managers with ease.

Enjoy the journey!

Disclaimer of Liability – This book is not about 'dictating' to the reader what they should or shouldn't be doing in respect of their business. Rather in utmost good faith and with much goodwill it offers (only) proven ways to improve the functioning of a business; ways/practices/processes which are based on my first-hand experiences. It is completely at the discretion of the reader as to what content of this book the reader chooses to be influenced by and act upon, and any risks or liabilities related to the reader adopting/acting upon any content of this book to suit their particular purposes are solely those of the reader to consider and bear.

2.0   New Business Start-up

This section presents key practical considerations to keep foremost in mind when starting-up a new business – from business idea conception to launch.

2.1 Hatching Your Business Idea

One of <u>the</u> most exhilarating moments of your life can be when that glorious idea pops itself into your head, which could be the result of a clear-headed "light bulb moment" or the result of having spent 8 consecutive nights tossing and turning in bed with little or no sleep.

 A "great business idea" need not be entirely brand new or original. It could (for example) represent a variation of (even an improvement upon) a commercial product/ service that is already known to be enjoying considerable success.

Whatever your idea is, make sure you:

1. Write it down/ type it into your electronic device.

2. (only if you feel the <u>absolute</u> need to) Share it with only your <u>most</u> trusted family member or friend. This person must have seriously high integrity and be highly trusted by you.

3. Do not share your idea with your wider family or circle of friends.

I advocate that you in fact keep your idea strictly to yourself until you have "hatched" your idea into a formal Strategic Plan.

Remember, the idea that you have been struck with to base a business on is no more and no less than a (seemingly) "great business idea" until you have prepared a written Strategic Plan to only then determine its potential commercial viability. Privately celebrate its conception – sure, yet it is advisable that you keep a lid on your excitement until you have fully rationalized your great idea by completing a written Strategic Plan.

There are three very good reasons not to share your idea with <u>any</u> other person:

a) As much as you have trusted your family member/ friend to date with all that has been sacred to you, you just never know what "loose lipped moment" they may succumb to when they're with other people – and before you know it your great idea has become someone else's great idea.

b) Your much trusted family member/friend may see your great idea as their ticket to fame and fortune, and set-out developing it as "their" great idea – launching it into the public arena ahead of you.

c) It can prove more difficult – and sometimes impossible – to successfully register a Patent in relation to an invention (e.g. product or service or system) if the invention has been shared with other people <u>prior</u> to the inventor applying to the relevant intellectual property organization (e.g. Intellectual Property Office of New Zealand, in the case of New Zealand) for a Patent.

2.2 The Essential Steps to Take to Start-up Your Business

2.2.1 Prepare Your Written Strategic Plan and Annual Business Plan

Having hatched your idea to base a business on, the very next step to take is to write a fully considered Strategic Plan.

This plan (note: many different Strategic Plan templates are offered freely via the internet) can be as detailed or as simple as you wish to make it, although I highly recommend that your Strategic Plan includes the following core elements:

1. Identify and clearly articulate what problem/

issue/ need your product or service will resolve for the people who you envisage will be interested in buying your product/service.

    a. What benefits will your product/ service provide.

    b. What problem/ issue/ need will your product/ service resolve.

    c. How will your product / service resolve the identified customer problem/ issue/ need.

    d. Is there a niche for your product/ service – and if so, what other players (competitors) have also seen this niche and/ or are already operating in this space.

    e. What will the Core Value Proposition (CVP) of your business be. That is, what value exactly will your product(s)/ service(s) provide target customers with.

2. Identify and define your target market(s).

    a. Define the profile of each primary set of target customers; in terms of (for example) their socio-economic status, their known preferences for the type of product/ service that you are considering offering, their personality (e.g. discerning, astute, etc), reasons why they would engage with your product/ service.

    b. You may discover that there is more than one primary target   market, because (for example) your product/ service has the potential to resolve more than one problem/ issue/ need.

    c. Define <u>how</u> your product/service would resolve the identified needs of each market segment.

3. Define exactly what your product/ service is.

    a. What are its features.

b. What are its benefits to each of the target market segments you identified.

c. What are its Unique Selling Points (USP's).

d. What are its limitations.

e. To what extent is it original versus a variation of an existing product/service.

4. Describe how your product/ service is to be produced/ delivered.

a. To what extent does the product rely on another party's products/ componentry parts.

b. What elements need to be manufactured internally versus externally.

c. What process needs to be followed in order to derive the finished product, and what costs are expected to be borne along the way.

5. SWOT Analysis. Be ruthless and truthful about identifying:

a. Strengths – of both the specific product/ service under consideration and in relation to the business model/operation/resource base as a whole.

b. Weaknesses – of both the specific product/service under consideration and in relation to the business model/operation/ resource based as a whole.

c. Opportunities – identify what "doors of opportunity" are likely to open as a consequence of launching the product/service under consideration as well as those opportunities generally which you anticipate lying ahead for your business.

d. Threats – in relation to both the specific product/service under consideration and in respect of the business model/operation/resource base as a whole. Include a comprehensive competitor analysis to determine estimated market share per business (including your own).

6. Strategic objectives. High level objectives/ goals which set the overarching direction for your business. Such objectives focus more on stating <u>what</u> your "big picture" commercial aspirations are – and <u>why</u> you have these aspirations; versus expressing the specific operational actions thought necessary in order to achieve the stated objectives (i.e. "how" the objectives would be pursued and met).

Examples of <u>Strategic</u> Objectives:

a. To increase overall market share from 15 % to 18 % by 2025.

b. To design and develop a world class ecommerce website which reflects proven best practice in the ecommerce realm by 2015.

c. To increase the leadership capabilities of the business owner, to ensure clear signs of   a positive work culture developing can be seen from January 2017.

d. To design and develop a customised training programme to be implemented   by Feb 2018, which will meet the professional development needs of all production personnel.

e. To develop written Operating Procedures for all of the key functions of the business by Dec 2016, to   achieve a good   level of cross-skilling across all personnel and to free-up management personnel so that they can concentrate more time on performing forward planning activities.

Both Strategic Plan and Business Plan (see further on) objectives should be:

- Specific

- Measureable

- Achievable

- Realistic

- Timely

7. Identify the range of resources required in order to meet your specified strategic objectives. Where human resources are concerned, identify:

- ➤ The specific functions that need to be fulfilled – and give these functions titles.

- ➤ The broad scope of each function (later these may be used to generate the detailed "Role Description" pertaining to each function).

- ➤ The approximate market rate of remuneration reflective of engaging the right person to fulfill each function.

Also identify:

- Technology resources thought necessary.

- Equipment thought necessary.

- Financial resources thought necessary. For example, to fund Research & Development.

8. Identify the best legal and operating structure/ model for the business.

Legal structure options include: sole trader, limited liability company, partnership and public company. Where choice of legal structure is concerned, think about:

➤ What personal financial risk do I want to expose myself/ my family to.

➤ Will my preferred legal structure readily enable me to invite new capital investment if/ when I want to consider increasing the scale of the business.

➤ What is my appetite and capability to act in a governance capacity.

➤ What need do I have to bring other people into the business, to ensure that skills/ strengths which I don't have are assigned to key functions which are outside the realm of my expertise.

Where the operating structure is concerned, think about:

➤ What (realistically) are my commercial strengths and weaknesses, and therefore what skills/ knowledge do I need to bring into the business in the form of: employees/ consultants/financial partners/ shareholders.

➤ Am I more orientated towards/ passionate about delivering the product/ service in my business (i.e. being an accomplished technician) or instead is running the business what really "spins my wheels" and is something that I have all/ most of the necessary knowledge/ skills to perform well at.

➤ What systemization (electronic and other) and processes will best ensure a smooth-running operation.

➢ What documentation needs to be in place to ensure that my operating structure is robust/ sound (e.g. written Shareholder Agreement, Operating Procedures, etc).

➢ Employee professional development – training programmes/ courses required to ensure that the team remains up-to-date with evolving practices/ industry trends.

9. Expected expenses/ costs that are likely to be incurred as a consequence of the business operating in accordance with your chosen legal and operating structure/ model.

Identify all of the foreseeable costs/ expenses that you deem are likely to arise, given the legal and operating structures you have chosen, and start to put broad financial projections ($ amounts) next to these, per Financial Year that is covered by the timeframe scope of your Strategic Plan.

If you will be operating out of a bricks and mortar site, then it is likely your operating costs will include:

- ➤ Rent

- ➤ Electricity

- ➤ Internet connectivity

- ➤ Telecommunications

- ➤ Stationery

- ➤ Etc

10. Broadly state what your succession plan looks like.

Even if you are anticipating investing significant time/ effort/ energy working in/ on your business for the next 15 – 20 years, it is useful to project forward and ask yourself the pivotal question of...

"What do I want the level of my involvement in my business to be x number of years from now?"

For example, it may be that 10 years from now you don't want to have any hands-on involvement working "in" your business, yet would still like to have equity in your business as a shareholder in order to continue to receive income from the business in the form of profit distributions.

It is important to <u>start</u> articulating (in broad terms) what your succession plan looks like, in your Strategic Plan. This discipline will help you remain mindful of the need to commit to your chosen succession plan as time goes on, and eventually your succession plan should appear in the <u>Business Plan</u> for the relevant Financial Year that marks the beginning of <u>implementing</u> your succession plan.

11. (Optional) Incorporate your Marketing Plan/ Strategy within your Strategic Plan

It is not uncommon for businesses to include their Marketing Strategy as a distinct section <u>within</u> their overarching Strategic Plan, rather than prepare a separate Marketing Plan document. I favour incorporating Marketing Strategy within the Strategic Plan, to then achieve a consolidated single document.

I highly recommend that your Marketing Strategy should include the following core elements:

a) Statement of current brand positioning.

b) Review of current brand and tag line effect/ relevancy.

c) Brand positioning objectives.

d) Statement as to what the essence of the brand is.

e) Identification of your target customers/ market segments (this would already be covered in your overarching Strategic Plan).

f) Identification of the need to perform market research to validate customer perception of your business/ products/ services...and especially customer perceived value of what you're offering relative to the price that you're attaching to your products/ services.

g) Product brands – what are they and what fundamental story do you wish to communicate to target customers about them.

h) How will your products/ services be delivered to target customers (e.g. bricks and mortar store).

i) What marketing channels will be used to expose your products/ services to target customers (e.g. bricks and mortar store, website, social media sites, magazines, etc).

j) What your pricing strategy is per product category/ brand.

k) What collaborative marketing activities could be undertaken working with one or more likeminded strategic partner.

Once you have prepared your Strategic Plan (note – typically Strategic Plans reflect a 3 year timeframe, yet some businesses like to consider 5 years ahead), you are then in a position to translate your Strategic Plan into your annual <u>Business Plan</u>.

Your annual Business Plan is where you commit to focusing on one or more strategic objective stated in your Strategic Plan, and write what are called "tactical" objectives in reflection of the chosen strategic objectives. These tactical objectives address <u>how</u> the given strategic objectives are to be achieved in a <u>practical/ operational</u> sense.

For example, if a strategic objective is…

"To increase overall market share from 15 % to 18 % by 2025" …then the <u>tactical</u> objective stated in the Business Plan could be…

To secure between 15 % - 18 % of the XYZ market by concentrating on increasing sales in respect of the following product categories:

- ABC Product Category – increase annual sales achievement by 5 % p.a. for the next 3 consecutive years.

- DEF Product Category – increase annual sales achievement by 7 % p.a. for the next 3 consecutive years.

...by increasing the amount of marketing budget devoted to increasing awareness/ visibility of these product categories to $x p.a. for the next 3 consecutive years.

Business Plan templates are available from a number of sources online now. Simply enter the keywords "Business Plan Template" in your favourite web browser Search Engine (e.g. Google) to uncover a template that suits your purposes. Ideally, see if the template can be downloaded and (once populated with your entries) saved as a .pdf file. By producing your plan as a (locked) .pdf file this will enable you to easily share your completed Business Plan with trusted parties who you need to show your Business Plan to in order to do things like obtain expert objective opinions on the validity and viability of your Business Plan and/or if you need to support your application for loan finance with empirical evidence of what the borrowed funds would be used for.

Essentially, your Business Plan is about qualifying and quantifying those strategic objectives that you wish to concentrate on pursuing during the relevant Financial Year which lies ahead. Your Business Plan should encapsulate all of your definitive financial projections for the Financial Year ahead, sufficient for you to use these projections to create your Profit & Loss (Income Statement) complete with forecast $ amounts (provisions).

2.2 .2 Market Research

It is surprising how many businesses overlook staying attuned to the needs/ desires of the people who they deem to be their target market.

There are essentially two different types of businesses – those which are production-driven and those which are marketing-led.

Production-driven businesses tend to have a mindset of "we know what our customers want, and we'll produce a product/ service that we know should meet their expectations".

On the other hand, marketing-led businesses tend not to speculate what customer do or don't want, by instead reaching out to target customers to determine their needs with greater certainty.

Marketing-led businesses tend to be more successful overall, simply for the reason that their products/ services tend to be more aligned to the needs of their target customers – because they commit to remaining in synch with what their target customers are saying they actually want/ expect/ desire in terms of the value proposition of the given product/ service.

I advocate that all businesses should perform two forms of market research as an inherent part of their business activity:

a) **Strategic Plan Customer Survey** – as a core part of setting the strategic direction of your business every 3 – 5 years, create a survey questionnaire which can either be distributed to a customer database and/ or used to perform face-to-face short interviews with customers.

I advocate using both methods (face-to-face interviewing and the distribution of the same questionnaire to a database of customers). The face-to-face interview process will draw-out greater emotion – and therefore sometimes different insights – from participants, versus responses provided by recipients of the written questionnaire.

The key insights that you are wanting to gain are:

- How (through what channels) does the customer prefer to connect with your business?

- How does the customer view your business, compared to your competitors' businesses?

- What value does the customer perceive exists in the product(s)/ service(s) that your business offers – especially in relation to price ?

- Does the customer consider there to be gaps in your product/ service mix?

- How does the customer rate their engagement experience in relation to your business – is it rewarding/ uplifting or otherwise?

- If the respondent doesn't currently connect with your business – what are the reasons they choose not to?

Use the findings from your market research to shape your Marketing Strategy for next 3 – 5 year planning timeframe, in respect of:

➢ Your product/ service offer – including what the points of difference will be.

➢ How you connect target customers with your business and product/ service offer (i.e. the specific marketing channels to use), to build brand awareness, strengthen customer engagement and more strongly influence a greater volume of successful sales occurring.

➢ Your pricing strategy – per product/ service category.

➢ How you distribute your product(s)/ service(s) – physical domain/ online domain.

b) Pre-Product/ Service Launch Market Validation
Having conceptualized a new product/ service that you're contemplating launching (ideally you may have perhaps even created a prototype), take the time to validate what you deem are the compelling features/attributes/benefits of the new product/service by holding Focus Group

sessions with one or more set of customers who you deem to be your target market(s).

Fundamentally, you are interested in learning:

- What features/elements of the product/ service does the Focus Group like – and why ?

- What features/elements don't they like – and why not ?

- Does the price that you are considering assigning to the given product/ service seem to be fair and reasonable to the Focus Group of target customers? Or instead, do they consider that a different price should apply, given their perception of the value of the product/ service that you are wanting to offer?

You may improve your hit/miss rate (and development costs) significantly by testing what customers think about your pending new product/ service before you commit to commercializing it (e.g. committing to the mass production run of a particular product).

This market validation phase may well also result in an improved sell-through rate if/when your product/service indeed becomes a commercial reality.

2.2.3 Register Your Trading Name (where relevant)

If you choose to establish your business as a company, then you will need to <u>register</u> it as such an entity (in New Zealand this is done with the NZ Companies Office).

What many businesses fail to then do is <u>also</u> register their business trading name (which may reflect the legal name of the business or instead an entirely different name as per what the business trades as in the public domain) as key intellectual property with the relevant IP registration authority (in N.Z. this is the Intellectual Property Office of N.Z.).

What typically influences a business owner to proceed to register their business trading name as their intellectual property is when they are asked to consider a scenario whereby a new entrant into the market sector that they operate in decides to assign the same trading name to their business – and upon doing so starts to attract customers away from the pre-existing business of the same trading name. Also, because significant Goodwill stemming from the trading name of a business can be factored into the selling price of a business if/ when the owner decides to sell their business as a going concern, if one or more other business shares the same trading name this may dilute the value of Goodwill that the incoming new owner is prepared to pay accordingly.

It has been proven that a business is likely to enjoy greater success defending a legal case involving another party having assumed/ taken the trading identity (or significant parts thereof) of the pre-existing business, where the pre-existing business had registered their trading name as a Trade Mark with the relevant authority beforehand.

The same prudent step should also be taken in relation to any unique/ novel tag line that a business creates in support of its trading identity, for marketing purposes.

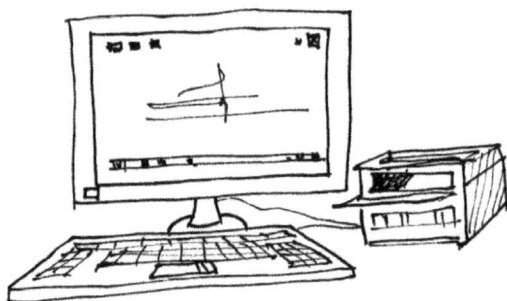

2.2.4 Register Your Products (where relevant)

Similarly, should you consider your product(s)/ service(s) to have unique/novel qualities (e.g. design/functionality/materials used, etc) – and/or the brands used to market/promote them reflect unique/novel elements, then it would be wise to consider registering this intellectual property with the relevant authority (again, in New Zealand this organization is the Intellectual Property Office of New Zealand and detailed IP registration information can be found in this website:

https://www.iponz.govt.nz/).

Products/ product features are typically registered in the form of a Design Registration and/or a Patent; whereas brands are typically registered as Trade Marks.

2.2.5 Establish a Shareholder Agreement (where relevant)

It is interesting to discover the number of companies (particularly small companies consisting of say a husband and wife) that still operate with no written Shareholder Agreement.

Over the years I have seen many (seemingly easily avoidable) disputes arise simply because no written Shareholder Agreement was in place to guide the resolution/treatment of relevant contestable situations. With no such framework in place decisions become contestable and prone to dispute between shareholders – particularly where equal voting rights prevail between shareholders.

When a husband and wife business ownership situation has presented itself to me, more often than not the husband and wife justify the absence of a Shareholder Agreement on the basis that each has their own designated (unwritten) responsibilities within the given business, and conflict and arguing doesn't occur between them. They don't envisage that there will ever be a time when either of them won't be willing to settle even seemingly irreconcilable differences between them.

I then convey my stories about husband and wife joint business ownership "bust-ups" – which often occur due to reasons/ circumstances that have arisen outside of the business – which (because of the absence of a written Shareholder Agreement) have resulted in the business being wound-up (dissolved) in order to incorporate the realized value of the business assets in the matrimonial property settlement.

My suggestion is, even if a husband and wife are the only shareholders of the business, from the outset (i.e. as an inherent part of establishing the business) put a (signed) written Shareholder Agreement in place.

The internet offers a range of different Shareholder Agreement templates, and solicitors are usually happy to guide the creation of a Shareholder Agreement and/ or even provide a template in some cases. However, whatever basis for your Shareholder Agreement you elect to use, it is highly advisable that you have your nominated solicitor evaluate what you deem to be the finalized document, before it is executed.

Protecting Your Interests When Poised to Start (or Expand) a Company –

If you have operated as a Sole Trader to date and are now wanting to establish your business under a company structure in order to perhaps engage one or more suitably skilled person to work alongside you (as a fellow shareholder) to strengthen your operation, it is highly advisable that you create the Shareholder Agreement <u>ahead</u> of inviting the relevant person/ people to join you.

This will ensure that you:

   a) Can provide evidence to the incoming shareholder(s) that indeed the contemplated company will have <u>proper structure</u> — a feature that should build confidence with prospective shareholders to contribute their time/ expertise and financial resources to the business.

b) Specify the fundamental "ground rules" where setting shareholder responsibilities and rights are concerned...and therefore avoid having to originate such provisions through a lengthy negotiation process per shareholder who joins your business.

Similarly, if you have operated as say a small company to date (e.g. husband and wife being the only shareholders), and you now wish to bring-in one or more additional shareholder who is/ are suitably skilled so as to strengthen your operation, then it is also highly advisable that you create the Shareholder Agreement <u>in advance</u> of inviting their shareholder interest — for the above key reasons.

2.2.6 Establish a Company Constitution (where relevant)

A Company Constitution sets out the powers, right and duties of: the company, the Board of Directors, each Director and each Shareholder. Company Constitution templates are readily available via the internet.

Most commonly (in New Zealand at least) it is the larger companies that often see merit in establishing a Company Constitution to add greater structure to their operation – i.e. over and above a Shareholder Agreement. In the case of smaller-medium sized companies, shareholders will often look to negate the need for a Company Constitution by including as many relevant provisions as possible that they would consider would otherwise appear in a Company Constitution, in the Shareholder Agreement instead; and/or rely on the provisions of statutory law to guide governance processes/decisions.

It is not mandatory in New Zealand for a company – irrespective of size/ scale of operation – to operate with a Company Constitution. In New Zealand, the provisions of the Companies Act 1993 prevail by default where a company does not have a Company Constitution in place.

In New Zealand, whatever provisions/ terms a company agrees to feature in its Company Constitution its Company Constitution cannot serve to contract that company out of its responsibilities as set out in the Companies Act 1993.

2.2.7 Establish Business Livery Protocols

Having spent often thousands of dollars developing a business and/ or product brand, many businesses don't then create a formal framework which guides how the brand is to be applied in the public domain – in the range of marketing channels and to the range of marketing collateral that the business elects to use.

So, unfortunately what happens in the absence of such a framework is that the brand can:

a) Be used in ways/ applied to channels that were not intended.

b) Be modified in appearance/ design/ scale to suit specific marketing mediums/ channels.

So what many commercially astute business owners do – particularly those who are interested in preserving the integrity of their business brand – is prepare what are commonly termed **"Corporate Identity Protocols"**.

These protocols:

- Show the official brand – including its official design, colouring, font, etc

- Show what the official tag line (if any) is – including font, colouring, scale relative to the brand, etc

- Show definitively all of the various applications that the brand (and tagline) is permitted to be used for – e.g. vehicle signage, store signage, stationery, website design, social media site design, presentation templates, etc – and exactly <u>how</u> the brand (and tagline) should be applied in each case.

If your business uses an intranet to store/ post company files, your intranet would be a good place for your Corporate Identity Protocols to be stored/ accessed from.

2.2.8 Appoint Professional Advisors

Depending on what your skill set is, it may be necessary for you to appoint either an Accountant and/ or a Solicitor to act in your interests.

A solicitor is typically engaged by a business owner to:

- Write/ evaluate legal documents such as Shareholder Agreement, Contract for Services Agreement, Company Constitution, Employment Agreement, Merger Agreement, etc.

- Provide guidance in respect of particularly complex employee-employer working relationship issues.

- Assist with problematic debt protection/ collection situations.

- Assist with the enforcement of Agreements.

- Provide support/ advice in relation to a business owner's re-structure proposal.

An Accountant is typically engaged by a business owner to:

- Help set-up a Chart of Accounts for the business – to thereby make the coding of transactions clear to perform and track through the accounting process.

- Prepare and submit GST Returns.

- Prepare End of Year Tax Returns.

- Prepare monthly Profit & Loss reports for the business owner to review and base decisions on.

- Prepare half-yearly and annual Financial Accounts.

- Provide guidance to the business owner in relation to how they may be able to rectify adverse financial outcomes.

Important –

When considering engaging an Accountant, I suggest that you make sure that the firm/person you engage is capable of providing you with services which extend <u>beyond</u> filing tax returns and preparing Financial Accounts.

Look to engage an Accountant who has the capability and willingness to perform a close analysis of your financial tracking/performance and report their insights/determinations to you in a clear manner which isn't littered with accounting jargon.

In my opinion what separates a great Accountant from a good Accountant is that a <u>great</u> Accountant will be able to tell you <u>why</u> the financial outcomes showing in your Profit & Loss/Balance Sheet are as they are, plus provide definitive advice as to <u>what you could conceivably do to change the given result</u>.

Make sure that your accounting software is easy to use, and generate reports from...and most importantly, will enable you to generate the range/ type of reports that you <u>need</u> to make decisions. In this Information Age that we are living in, your accounting software system should be able to not only report from General Ledger level up to Balance Sheet level, but should also be able to manage your inventory and payroll and enable cash flow management and reporting.

2.2.9 Identify Strategic Partners

Particularly for small-medium sized businesses, there are considerable benefits to be enjoyed from forming strong commercial relationships with one or more other business that is well-aligned to your own. I call these "Strategic Partnerships".

A "Strategic Partnership" is where two or more separate businesses (i.e. separate ownership) see sufficient merit in forming an alliance in order to achieve certain objectives. Such objectives could be:

- To promote complementary products in the public domain.

- To achieve exclusivity or some other special trading terms in relation to certain products/ services.

- To pool together funding for collaborative marketing purposes.

For example, during my time working as a CEO in the jewellery industry, the retail jeweller national franchise that I was working for established written "Preferred Supplier Agreements" with carefully selected suppliers. These Agreements provided for special supply, pricing and marketing terms of trade to be established between the chosen suppliers and the retailers who were their Business-to-Business customers.

Sometimes commercial collaboration can be achieved simply by working with a Strategic Partner to hold an event at which both parties are represented and have the opportunity to pitch to the audience which has gathered.

In this case, the common ground for collaboration is most likely to be that the guests who are invited to the event are equally target customers of both businesses. Strategic Partnerships are not difficult to form. It is recommended (from experience) that business owners follow a path similar to this, when prospecting for new Strategic Partners:

Step One – write down exactly what you aim to achieve through engaging with the Strategic Partner(s) you have in mind. Also write down the goals that you think the partner would be looking to achieve through such a relationship.

Step Two – prepare a written pitch, which outlines what the collaboration opportunity is and what the benefits to each party would be likely to be.

Step Three – meet with the identified Strategic Partner prospect(s), and go through the pitch with them. Leave them with the pitch, for them to reflect upon.

Step Four – in the event the Strategic Partner confirms their wish to form a commercial partnership in accordance with the pitch/ proposal, then proceed to create a written Agreement which encapsulates the terms/relationship facets that have been agreed to date. Issue this document as a draft to the other party for their review and feedback, and once finalized both parties should sign this document before any implementation activity commences.

2.2.10 Develop An Annual Marketing   Activity Schedule & Associated Marketing Budget

Once you have finalized your written Marketing Strategy for your business, you are then in a position to use your Marketing Strategy to set your Marketing Activity Schedule for the first Financial Year reflected in your Marketing Strategy.

This step is about translating your elected marketing strategy into an <u>operational</u>- level framework which can be used as a "concrete" planning and management tool to <u>deliver</u> whatever marketing activity you have determined should apply during the up-and-coming Financial Year.

It is highly recommended that your Marketing Activity Schedule spans a Financial Year at a time, to enable any marketing service providers who you elect to engage to plan forward to accommodate your requirements in their own critical path.

Your Marketing Activity Schedule (which can readily be set-up as a spreadsheet) should feature these fields:

- **Marketing Activity Description** – e.g. distribution of Customer eNewsletter, creation of a DLE Flyer for in-store distribution, content created for Facebook site (include the focus, theme and nature of content, in your description), creation of a competition for website (include duration and the call-to-action that competition participants must perform in order to be eligible to win the prize, in your description), special event, etc.

- **Purpose of Marketing Activity** – define what outcome(s) you are wanting to see from implementing each scheduled marketing initiative. E.g. Increase the number of people who enter my store and/

or Increase the number of purchase orders received via my ecommerce website.

- **Launch Timing** – specify the date on which the given initiative should be launched live in the public domain.

- **Effective Timeframe** – specify the timeframe during which the given marketing initiative is to remain live in the public domain.

- **Marketing Provider** – specify which party will be engaged to produce the marketing initiative (for example it could be performed by specialist internal employees and/ or by a contracted marketing agency).

- **Estimated Cost** – enter the $ amount that you consider will be required to execute the marketing initiative. This amount will either reflect estimated time in attendance by the relevant internal employee and/or estimated time/cost that is thought likely to be incurred by the contracted marketing agency.

If you specified an objective in your Marketing Strategy to bolster sales during a typically slower/ sluggish trading time of the year when you haven't conventionally assigned any marketing budget to that time period historically, then make sure that your Marketing Activity Schedule indeed includes marketing initiatives for this timeframe in the forthcoming Financial Year.

Important -

Irrespective of whether you expect to engage an external marketing services provider to deliver at least some of the initiatives that you commit to your Marketing Activity Schedule, or not; it is highly advisable that you identify a credible well established/proven marketing services provider to meet with to present your Marketing Activity Schedule to them – so that they can:

a) Challenge the validity of what you have scheduled based on their knowledge of current proven effective marketing tactics.

b) Based on the total size of the available Marketing Budget, suggest a different allocation/ weighting of funding to each chosen marketing initiative, again based on their knowledge and prediction of what initiatives are more likely to have greater commercial effect than others.

c) Suggest reorganizing the timing of when particular events should launch, based on their knowledge of (for example) up-and-coming events which your initiative could conceivably dove-tail into, or in order to avoid particular occasions such as School Holidays (when sales are known to dip due for particularly product categories despite all reasonable marketing efforts applied).

d) Identify where – based on the cost estimations you have included in your Marketing Activity Schedule for internal employees to perform the execution of particular initiatives – they consider they would be able to execute the same initiative at a lower cost.

The key suggestion to make here is <u>be prepared to allow</u> such a specialist marketing services provider to critique your Marketing Activity Schedule, for you never know what improvements they may be able to suggest which result in a more effective use of your marketing funds.

Once you have finalized your Marketing Activity Schedule – which includes having had your cost estimates rationalized in order to have these estimates become as realistic/ accurate as possible, you are now ready to set-up your Marketing Budget for the same relevant Financial Year. Again this can be achieved simply by using a spreadsheet.

Your Marketing Budget tracks actual marketing expenditure incurred in comparison with the amounts that you had anticipated/predicted would be incurred, based on the range of marketing initiatives you committed to in your Marketing Activity Schedule.

The fields that should be present in your Marketing Budget should be:

Marketing Initiative – paraphrase a succinct description from your Marketing Activity Schedule sufficient for you to easily identify the nature of the given initiative.

Estimated Total Implementation Cost – enter the total cost that you   expect to incur in order to implement the given marketing initiative.

Months of the Financial Year (as column headings) – in reference to the 'Estimated Total Implementation Cost' amount, enter the relevant portion ($) of this total amount that you expect to be incurred in whatever month(s). This practice will help you manage your cash flow... and then as the Financial Year unfolds and you receive invoices for marketing services provided, enter each total invoice amount next to the relevant marketing initiative in the given month column(s) that the invoice relates to relates to. This will enable you track actual versus forecast marketing spend as the Financial Year unfolds, and therefore be in a position to alter certain planned marketing activities (scope/ budget allocation) depending on how closely actual marketing spend YTD (Year To Date) is tracking to forecast spend.

The 'Total YTD Marketing Spend' figure in your Marketing Budget should be the same figure as that which appears in relation to the field 'Advertising' (or whatever alternative General Ledger fieldname you have set-up to identify your marketing expenditure) in your Profit & Loss Report (Income Statement).

3.0 Involve Your Team in Brainstorming at Least Strategic Objectives

Over the years I can recall a number of business owners who have asked me why their well contemplated and beautifully prepared Strategic Plan has failed to win the support of the given owner's employee team. In response, I have asked the simple question, "at what stage of the planning process did you invite input from relevant people on your team?"

Typically, the business owner answered either that they didn't invite any input from their team throughout the time the Strategic Plan was being written, or that such an invitation was communicated only when the plan had been written and was being presented to the team for their feedback.

And therein lies the reason why the troops may show a lackluster appreciation when being presented with a business owner's well-crafted Strategic Plan...no matter how professionally put together the plan may be and/ or no matter how valid the content may be.

Unless a business owner/ senior manager (e.g. CEO/ GM) makes the choice to involve relevant members of their team at the early stages of formulating a Strategic Plan (irrespective of whether the business is a start-up venture or has been trading for some time), they cannot expect their team members to feel any great sense of "buy-in" (ownership) in relation to the plan once it is finalized.

Where instigating change is concerned, I have found that most people prefer to be a part of formulating the change versus having the change inflicted upon them. Furthermore, I have found that the greatest sense of ownership of strategic direction that you (as a business owner/senior manager) can influence in anyone occurs when the people concerned have been an integral part of the planning process from the <u>outset</u>.

4.0 Share the Finalised Plan with Relevant Team Members

As a business owner/senior manager, if you expect your team to follow your lead as you embark upon the journey that you have mapped-out in your Strategic Plan, then it is imperative that you <u>share</u> the finalise plan with your team.

Over the years I have seen considerable disconnection between business owners/senior managers and the internal stakeholders who they are leading, simply because of their failure to share key information about the chosen direction of the given company.

While it isn't necessary to publish the Strategic Plan verbatim to relevant parties, sharing of most particularly the strategic objectives with these parties

- in whatever summary format is deemed necessary - should greatly improve the chances of these stakeholders working in accordance with what the chosen direction is.

I have often heard comments of frustration expressed by business owners/senior managers, along the lines of "they just don't seem to understand what I'm wanting the business to achieve". More often than not, the main reason for this frustration has simply been an oversight on the business owner's/senior manager's part to communicate key elements of the Strategic Plan to these people – which would have served to enlighten them as to what was expected of them going forward.

5.0 Fine Tune Your First Business Unit Before Expanding

I have seen a few cases of (perhaps) overly-enthusiastic business owners wanting to increase their market representation as quickly as possible after reaching a critical mass/breakeven trading position. Their expansion aspirations have mainly taken the form of wanting to open additional bricks and mortar branches or franchise their model.

In my view, it is not sensible to implement such an expansion plan until such time that the existing operation (i.e. single business unit) has been streamlined to the best of the owner's capability – including: electronic systems, operating procedures and internal policy most importantly.

If shortcomings/glitches/bugs/omissions are known to exist in relation to the existing business unit, then by establishing additional sites/branches which are more or less replicas of the existing model, the same issues are going to present themselves...only now you are faced with having to "put out the fires" in relation to both the existing business and the new site(s).

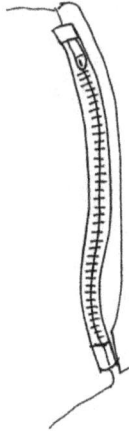

6.0 Merging is a Plausible Option to Achieve Growth, Stability and New Opportunities

Sometimes, in order for a business to remain viable or achieve desired strategic objectives (e.g. create a more affordable and sustainable operating structure) it can make great sense for that business to consider merging its commercial interests with that of another business which offers appealing features (e.g. scale of operation, certain complementary product/ service offerings, certain specialty human resources, similar culture, etc).

Often it only takes an initial conversation between representatives of two companies to know what the "common ground" - and strength of interest of each party - is.

Important –

Where company mergers are concerned, I consider that the single most important factor which both parties must see firm evidence of before advancing discussions to any formal conclusion is the extent to which the <u>culture</u> of both companies is <u>aligned</u>/ similar.

While it is a relatively straightforward matter for the systems/ operating procedures/ assets/ intellectual property of two companies to be brought together and rationalized as to which will be continued versus discontinued with, I have found that it is the extent to which the <u>culture</u> of the respective organizations <u>align</u> that will determine an overall successful merger outcome or not. To this end, I highly recommend that as a part of early merger discussions, the two parties spend a good amount of time discussing their respective culture – and in particular the cultural elements that they each expect/ want to <u>retain</u> once the entities have merged.

PARENT COMPANY

SHAREHOLDER COMPANY *1.

SHAREHOLDER COMPANY *2.

SHAREHOLDER COMPANY *3.

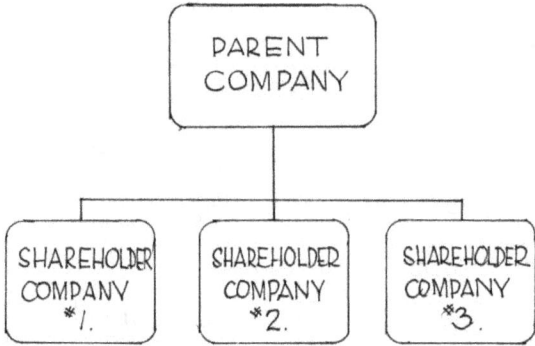

7.0 Collaboration of Aligned Entities Under a Single Parent Company

Sometimes it makes good sense for multiple businesses which share a common interest to operate under a single Parent Company – and therefore trade in the public domain under a single business brand. For example, it may be that a small marketing agency has formed close working relationships with a small website design agency, a Copywriter, and a small SEO (Search Engine Optimization) agency. All of these entities operate in the marketing realm, yet each individually trades under their own business brand and achieves a small annual revenue stream only.

The marketing agency owner decides to hold a meeting with the owners of the other businesses to propose that they combine their respective resources under the structure of a single Parent Company and trade under a single business brand - a proposal which is agreed to by the other business owners.

Each of the small businesses is a Limited Liability Company in its own right. The inaugural meeting of these business owners results in a Shareholder Agreement relating to the Parent Company being adopted and executed by all of the small business owners – making each of them a shareholder of the new Parent Company. The Shareholder Agreement contains key provisions such as:

- Shareholder investment contributions

- Shareholder rights and shareholder responsibilities

- Treatment of any assets/ IP contributed to the Parent Company by shareholders

- ...and any other provisions that the shareholders of the newly-formed

Parent Company agree to feature in the Shareholder Agreement.

Depending on the size (number of shareholders) of the Parent Company – plus the range and nature of provisions featured in the Parent Company Shareholder Agreement, shareholders may also choose to bring a Company Constitution into effect – which adds further rigidity to the structure of the Parent Company. The Company Constitution could include provisions such as: process for conducting a Share Buy-back, director rights and responsibilities, shareholder meeting processes, distribution of end of year profit, etc.

During the time that I was serving as a Business Advisor in the Hawke's Bay region (New Zealand), I worked with a small set of businesses which operated in the same professional industry to help them understand the benefits of their respective small practices becoming shareholders of a Parent Company. These benefits included:

- The individual business units would cease being competitors and would become comrades, working in the same common direction in accordance with the Parent Company Strategic Plan.

- It would enable them to relieve one-another whenever one professional is sick or wishes to go on holiday.

- It would enable pooling of financial resources to be able to afford to purchase the most up-to-date equipment needed, and a proper marketing programme.

- Invoicing of clients could be achieved through a Central Billing function – resourced by 1 – 2 administration employees; rather than have at least 1 admin person per individual professional practice processing invoices.

- It would create the opportunity to successively attract more professional practices to join the Parent Company model over time, and then perhaps justify the appointment of a General Manager to pursue attracting further new shareholder interest as well as oversee the operation – from accounts to marketing to legal compliance.

- The professional practitioners could focus their time/energy/effort on the delivery of their professional services only, and leave the running of the business to an appointed, suitably skilled person such as a General Manager.

The key to forming a Parent Company which will deliver the benefits that its shareholders aspire to receive, is ensuring that a good level of <u>trust and mutual respect</u> already exists between the individuals who are destined to be the shareholders of pending Parent Company. These essential ingredients will help shareholder decision-making considerably, and keep internal political "disturbances" to a minimum.

The beauty of the kind of Parent Company structure above is that in the event that one or more shareholder wishes to cease being a shareholder of the Parent Company for whatever reason and at whatever stage, then they can simply terminate their involvement with the Parent Company and resume trading under their own trading identity (business brand) under their own Limited Liability company structure.

8.0 Strive to Be Customer Centric and Marketing Led in All That You Do .

The most successful businesses on the planet are mostly those that are <u>marketing- led</u>, as opposed to being production-driven. Such businesses make it a core part of their business to <u>maintain a current understanding</u> of what the needs/ desires/ expectations of target customers are to then put themselves in an informed position to make well-reasoned judgements as to:

a) What products/services to provide – and the features/attributes of these products/ services.

b) How best to connect target customers with their business – what marketing channels, collateral and communication to use.

c) How best to get their product(s)/service(s) in front of customers – physical and online sites.

d) What pricing to apply per product category, based on customer perceived value of the given product/ service offering.

By being customer-centric your business can look forward to the possibility of:

- Incurring less wastage where the manufacture of products is concerned.

- Achieving a higher sell-through rate for your products/services because your offer is more closely aligned to what customers are saying they want/need/expect.

- Achieving higher levels of customer engagement – through more people being able to see that what your business is offering is what they actually want/ need/ desire.

- Composing Marketing Strategy and annual Marketing Activity Schedules that are more attuned to the marketing channel/ collateral preferences of your target market(s).

Over the years I have come across many businesses which operate with a "we know what's best for our customers" or "we know what our customers want" attitude; which causes them to essentially push product into the market relying on little more than historic sell-through data to guide their product/ service delivery.

The problem with this mindset is that their future product/ service delivery proposition may be governed by <u>historic</u> customer demand trends; which means that the likelihood of such a business expanding its market share may be slim because they're failing to entertain emerging new trends in their sector of operation.

Whereas the proactive (marketing-led) business is continuously monitoring and interacting with the market (through performing market research) to most particularly:

i) Understand how well their current product/service offering is aligned to target customer needs.

ii) Learn what target customers both like and dislike about their product/ service offering.

iii) Learn how customers prefer to connect with their business – i.e. the marketing channels that they favour using.

See earlier in this book for effective and affordable ways to perform market research, in order to stay well aligned to your target customer needs.

9.0 Make Your Business as Process and Systems Orientated as Possible From the Outset

Particularly if your business is a small business and you're starting-up, it will prove critical for you to introduce reliable processes and systems into your business as early-on as possible if you are to release yourself from the more mundane "coalface" activities in order to work <u>on</u> evolving your business – for it to grow and gain more market share.

One of the key reasons why small businesses remain as small businesses is that the owners fail to create suitable structure (in terms of well-defined processes and systems) around how the day-to-day activities of the business are to be performed.

A fantastic way of injecting robust structure into your business is to ensure that you have a <u>written Operating Procedure</u> in place for each key function that is required to be performed.

Operating Procedures are a <u>key</u> tool to use to:

a) Set your team up to win. I believe that no person deliberately sets-out to do a "bad job" or work at odds with an employer's expectations. Rather, I think it is more the case that when an undesirable outcome (i.e. an outcome which is not in-line with someone else's expectations) occurs as a result of a person's action or inaction, the person who set the framework for the work delivery failed to communicate clearly enough what was expected of the other person/ people. And by doing so, it was <u>they</u> who were actually responsible for setting the other person/ people up to lose (fall short of expectations).

b) Ensure that your business can continue to function well even if a person who is normally the designated expert to perform a certain role is away sick or on holiday.

c) Encourage the cross-skilling of members of your team who show an interest in wanting to learn a new role within the business. Operating Procedures provide these people with a reference point to refresh their memories as often as they like as to how a particular process/ function is expected to be performed.

d) Empower your team members – allow

them to "stand on their own two feet" and feel proud about working as autonomously as possible in their appointed position.

e) Free-up the business owner/ manager – for them to then be able to concentrate their time/ energies/ effort working on a project/ plan which is designed to evolve/ grow the business further.

The key to achieving effective Operating Procedures is four-fold, as follows:

a) Use "concrete" language – Plain English vocabulary which is generally understood by a 12 – 14 year old reader.

b) Use images/ graphics to support the written word – "a picture tells a thousand words"...and video is even better.

c) Make the wording succinct (to the point) using a direct communication style, and ensure that the document is structured as a procedural document (i.e. incorporates a style such as "Step One:" "Step Two", "Step

Three", etc.

c) Wherever possible, to ensure that the written word indeed reflects current best proven practice, involve the person who is presently fulfilling the given role, in the process of at least drafting the related Operating Procedure. This measure will help instill a sense of ownership of the finalized Operating Procedure with the incumbent.

d) If your business operates with an intranet, it would be a good idea to post your Operating Procedures in your intranet for ready access and download by authorized internal stakeholders. This is a particularly good idea where your team use a mobile device (e.g. iPad) as a routine part of their role – and can therefore look-up an Operating Procedure as often as they need to via the company's intranet.

"1+2+3 = SUCCESS!"

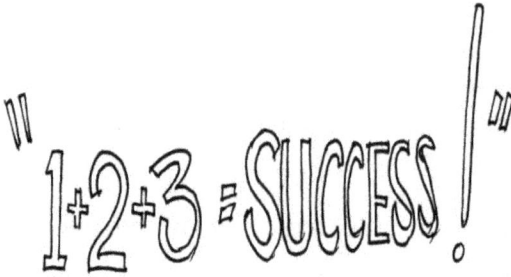

10.0 Determine the 'Critical Success Factors' of Your Business From the Outset

Too many times (particularly) small businesses fail to gain (or maintain) good momentum due to the owner(s) finding themselves erecting or fixing their structure <u>as they concurrently</u> pour time and energy into contributing towards the generation of revenue.

On each occasion where I have seen the above practice, the business concerned has typically been close to becoming dysfunctional in terms of:

- Communication breakdown

- Stakeholder relationship breakdown

- A company culture which is characterized by

distrust and disharmony

- Internal stakeholders threatening to "abandon the ship"

- Little-no sense of commercial direction, and a low level of purpose felt by internal stakeholders who are subordinate to the owners

If a builder builds the walls of a house without creating a robust foundation (concrete or piles), then the chances of the walls remaining unaffected by say an earthquake would be slim...which then of course compromises the balance of the features of the house.

A business is no different in respect of the need for a robust structure (foundation) to be in place if its operation is going to run as smoothly as possible and for the business to realise its commercial potential. These are the **Critical Success Factors** of an organization.

I have found that the following Critical Success Factors are common to most organizations (commercial and non-commercial alike):

i) The legal structure is correct, given what the owners' objectives and funding requirements are.

ii) The correct legal documentation in support of the chosen legal structure is in place. E.g. Shareholder Agreement, Company Constitution, Contract for Services Agreement, etc.

iii) Capital and working capital base is sufficient.

iv) A suitable IT system is in place to create a reliable and easy-to-use system for communication to flow readily amongst most particularly internal stakeholders.

v) A current written Strategic Plan is in place and is driving the operational delivery. And the strategy has been <u>shared</u> with relevant internal stakeholders who are instrumental in its delivery.

vi) A current written Marketing Strategy is in place and is driving the creation and implementation of marketing activity.

vii) A well written and up-to-date Operating Procedure is in place per key function.

viii) The right people with the right skill sets and competencies have been appointed to the range of identified functions/ roles.

ix) A well written and up-to-date Job/ Position description is in place per work role.

x) The accounting system engaged is easy-to-use and is capable of generating the range of clear reports that the relevant stakeholders need in order to make good decisions.

xi) The owners have either empowered a suitably qualified and skilled person to manage the day-to-day business operation on their behalf or they purposely schedule to work "on" the business at least one day each week, to enable them to address opportunities/ situations which have the potential to evolve the business – for it to grow and realise more market share.

xii) The owners and senior management team are client-centric, and market research features as a key component of their

Marketing Strategy ongoing.

xiii)   … and arguably most importantly, the owners are predisposed to being prepared to change (both themselves and aspects of their organization) as the need to change becomes apparent. They deeply understand the need for them (and their team) to keep <u>adapting</u> in order for their business to survive and (hopefully) thrive.

If you are contemplating establishing a new business, it is highly advisable that you achieve getting as many of the above Critical Success Factors in place as possible <u>before</u> you start trading.

Important Lesson to Learn –

If/when putting together a License Agreement to define the working relationship between a Licensor (yourself) and a Licensee, you run the very real risk that the people who you attract as Licensees develop only a "loose" sense of connection with the business and brand <u>if</u> the agreement doesn't provide for the Licensees to receive tangible benefit from the business during the years that they are a Licensee.

I have seen this happen, and to prevent the Licensees from becoming even more disenfranchised from the business concerned, I led a major review and overhaul of the relevant License Agreement so that the opportunity was created for Licensees to sell their own commercial interests in the business at a market rate of their determination if/ when they made the decision to exit the business.

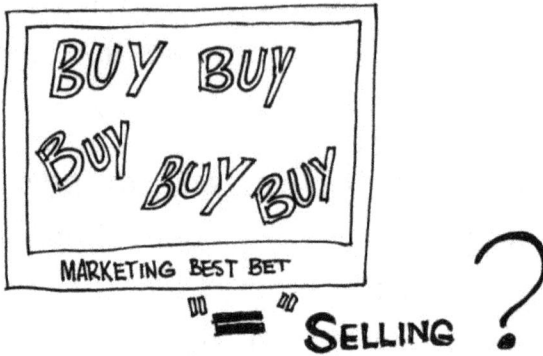

11.0 What 'Marketing' is – and What it Isn't

It is useful to create some clarity around what marketing actually is... First and foremost, marketing is not selling. The primary purpose of marketing is to instil such a need/desire within the hearts/minds of a target audience that the individuals become driven/ compelled to engage with the business(es) which will satisfy this need. Selling is the act of converting this need into a purchase transaction.

Marketing increases the potential for a successful sale to take place...but it is not ultimately responsible for the sale transaction eventuating.

Marketing sets the stage for a successful sales conversion (transaction) to transpire. The backbone of marketing is a model called the 'AIDA' model. This model (which has been around for literally decades) is widely referred to in many different resources – including Wikipedia; and tertiary education providers of marketing courses have done a great job for many years of teaching students what this important model means and how to apply it.

I have included a summary of my interpretation of the AIDA model in this book, for when I was performing as a Business Advisor and was explaining the usefulness of this model to business owners for their own marketing planning purposes, this model was embraced by these people as a "light bulb revelation" which they considered would assist them greatly when originating marketing collateral/ initiatives going forward.

My own opinion is that I consider the AIDA model to be the most valuable information that I came into while working my way through my Bachelor of Business Studies Degree. It has aided me countless times in writing marketing briefs and in helping businesses achieve a good return on the funds that they have devoted to implementing marketing activities/ initiatives.

The AIDA model:

- **A** – Attention (Awareness)
- **I** – Interest
- **D** – Desire
- **A** – Action

A – Attention (Awareness):

Effective marketing will – in the first instance - cause a person to become <u>aware</u> of what the message (or other marketing stimulus) is, and <u>attend</u> to it.

The <u>level</u> of awareness that results will depend on:

- The extent to which the marketing stimulus (e.g. billboard, signage, website, newspaper ad, etc) can be easily and quickly accessed and observed.

- The design characteristics of the marketing initiatives (e.g. use of colour, application of proven best design practices in web design, level of creativity, etc)

- The extent to which an observer is attracted to the stimulus – because it has "wow" factor and is well aligned to their tastes (i.e. the appeal that it has).

I – Interest:

If the marketing stimulus is powerful enough and is clear and easy to interpret, <u>interest</u> in what the marketing stimulus is presenting/ communicating will develop within the observer.

Marketers try to cause <u>interest</u> to develop within a few seconds (only) of awareness taking place.

Examples:

- Typical website visitor interest capture timeframe = 2 – 3 seconds

- Typical timeframe in which the interest of customers needs to be captured when they are passing by the front windows of a bricks and mortar store =

3 – 5 seconds

- Typical timeframe available for a printed ad (e.g. newspaper) to capture the interest of a reader = 2 – 3 seconds

Important: Marketers recognise that generally we are all busy people a lot of the time, and need to interpret information and make decisions quickly

D – Desire:

If the marketing stimulus is sufficiently powerful then interest will quickly transform into <u>desire</u> in the mind of the consumer. The skilled marketer knows the importance of influencing this feeling of desire to happen as quickly as possible - and this is where the <u>emotions</u> of the observer are "played upon" to instil desire.

Marketing stimulus which possesses a high level of emotional content (e.g. Valentine's Day television commercial featuring a man providing his partner with breakfast in bed) is purposely this way, to drive target audiences to <u>desire</u> the product/ service that the stimulus is communicating.

Generally, as research has determined repeatedly over the years, most people (particularly women) are influenced to proceed to purchase based on emotion...far more so than using rational logic.

A – Action:

The ultimate goal of the marketer is to instil such a sense of desire in the heart and mind of the targeted customer that it causes the customer to take action to relieve/satisfy the need that has built-up within them to experience what the marketing stimulus has told them they "need".

Example:

Action can take the form of the customer:

- making a phone call (TXT or email) to the business to ask questions/ seek clarification/ validation

- completing a booking or order form

- meeting a business representative face-to-face

- proceeding to enter the selling process (online or in a store)

I recommend that you use the AIDA model as a "filter":

a) When preparing a written marketing brief – to make sure that you ask your chosen marketing provider for features in the given marketing initiative that will "tick all of the boxes" in the AIDA model.

b) When creating marketing initiatives using your own internal resources – to make sure that what you're contemplating developing will "tick all of the boxes" in the AIDA model.

12.0 The Importance of a Multi-channel Marketing Strategy

Through performing market research (see section earlier in this book) in conjunction with setting your Marketing Strategy every 3 – 5 years, you will gain:

Useful insights as to what marketing channels your target customers prefer to use to connect with your business.

I have been interested to learn in recent times that despite the phenomenal growth in popularity of social media sites as mainstream communication vehicles, particularly people aged 40 years and upwards still enjoy engaging regularly with television and magazines (and a hardcopy newspaper in the weekend).

So, before you commit marketing initiatives to your annual Marketing Activity Schedule, do some research to know with some certainty what the preferred marketing channels of your target customers are.

Depending on what your own market research determines as being the preferred marketing channels used by your target customers, the following is an example (only) of a well-rounded range of marketing activity for a retailer who operates in both the bricks and mortar environment and online realm.

Bricks and Mortar -

- DLE flyer depicting a cross-section of products from the most recent collection – with the "brand story" included for each product brand featured. Flyer to be distributed in-store only.

- Adhesive label for store front window announcing the release of the given new collection of products.

- Poster/ banner of a size to suit the space available in the store front window reinforcing the given promotion theme.

- Gift bags which support the given promotion theme.

Online –

- Facebook social media site content – always with a link to the business's main website included.

- Instagram social media site (if main target customer segment is younger people) – link to blog in Blog website/product in eCommerce website.

- Blog website content. Ecommerce website – up-to-date SKU's.

Direct Marketing –

- Periodic electronic customer newsletter – distributed via the likes of Mailchimp.

Note – some businesses publish a customer newsletter every week, and some even twice a week. Monitor the "Unsubscribe" rate to learn what is an acceptable frequency from your customers' perspective. Always include a link to your website in your newsletter.

Traditional Media –

- Advertorial in a magazine publication which reflects your business brand positioning.

Important Lesson to Learn -

Some marketing agencies can charge a fairly hefty rate for their services. Apart from any base 'Agency Fee' that some agencies look to apply – particularly in those cases where the client has an in-depth long-term working relationship with them, marketing agencies will also charge per scope of work that they are asked to perform (i.e. per marketing initiative that is committed to your Marketing Activity Schedule). Therefore, if you want to avoid "surprise" invoice amounts from your chosen marketing services provider, when the time comes for the provider to implement any given scheduled marketing initiative it is highly advisable that you prepare a fully considered written brief for the work to be performed – and receive a <u>Quote</u> (as opposed to the estimated figure that you have been working with to date) – from the provider in return.

Many small businesses (in particular) make the choice of assigning responsibility for determining the creative scope of marketing initiatives to their favoured marketing agency…which then exposes these businesses to the possibility that their provider will need to generate <u>multiple</u> artwork/ storyboard scenarios (at your cost) before they finally produce a concept which suits your needs.

Whereas, if you instead devote some concentrated time to conceiving (even in broad terms) the kind of marketing collateral that you need/ want – and then commit these thoughts to a well written Marketing Brief, this should prove to reduce the amount of time that your provider will spend essentially "second-guessing" what you need/ want.

13.0 Be Disciplined at Reviewing Your Progress (Management Reporting)

In business it is <u>cash flow</u> that is king! It is ultimately cash flow stemming from the sales that your business achieves that determines whether you can settle creditor invoices, pay employee wages...and keep the business operating as a viable trading concern.

Therefore it is advisable that you maintain the discipline of reviewing your Cash Flow position at least once per week. To this end, create a Cash Flow Budget which will enable you to set Cash Flow forecasts and track actual Cash Flow into and out of your business bank account. Specialty software is available now to make this a straightforward exercise, and which integrates with at least the more popular mainstream accounting software systems.

A key objective as far as managing your Cash Flow is concerned, should be to minimize the number of occasions when you expect to have a negative cash flow position (and therefore must rely on any overdraft facility that you may have in place to help meet your cash flow commitments).

It is also advisable to review the tracking of your Operating Budget (Profit & Loss) each month, to learn what your overall trading position is – and to then know what adjustments you may need to make to forecast budget provisions in relation to one or more month ahead given what the YTD position is.

To repeat an important statement made earlier in this book, if you require the assistance of your Accountant to help you understand the figures presented in your Profit & Loss Report your Accountant should be able to not only say "what" the figures mean but also "why" they are as they are, and offer suggestions as to "how" you could conceivably improve particular outcomes during the coming months.

The key determination to make in relation to your monthly Profit & Loss review is whether or not your business is trading profitably (i.e. a YTD Net Profit is evident).

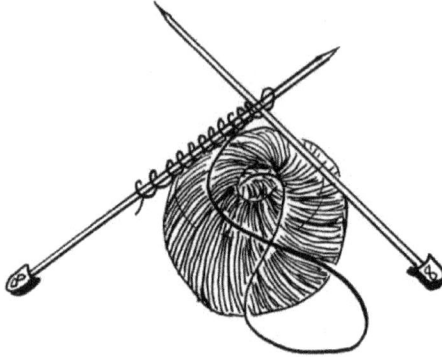

14.0 Be Disciplined at Sticking to Your Core Business

While a commendable growth strategy used by many businesses is to diversify their product mix, be careful as to the extent (and speed at which) you diversify. Product diversification typically means adding one or more new product to your existing offer...which generally requires a financial investment (e.g. for research & development, if the product is a new innovation).

<u>Before</u> you diversify your product mix, review your Cash Flow Budget to make sure that you can <u>realistically afford</u> to proceed with this action.

Also <u>before</u> you diversify your product/ service offering, think carefully about:

- What extra human resources would I need to have in place in support of the new products/ services under consideration?

- How would the introduction of the new product(s)/service(s) impact on how current customers perceive - and engage with - my business?

- Do I run the risk of alienating some customers due to their perception that I have changed the main focus of my business?

- To what extent would new customers be attracted to engage with my business?

There is no harm in diversifying your product/ service offering – for the additions to then become a part of your "Core Business", providing that you firstly thoroughly <u>rationalise</u> the implications (using prompts/questions such as those above) of diversifying <u>before</u> you proceed to do so.

Sometimes businesses that have attempted to diversify their product/service offer have found that the total number of customers who engaged with their business (or total sales $ achieved) <u>reduced</u> soon after making the change; an outcome which caused them to return to only offer what their core value proposition was prior to trialling their diversification strategy.

A key advantage of "sticking to your knitting" (i.e. your core business) is that you increasingly become a specialist at providing the product/service that you have chosen to remain focused on, and therefore become well known/regarded as such by customers – which can influence business growth.

15.0 No One Has a Monopoly on Good Ideas

One significant truism that I learnt early on as I stepped into the management realm is that <u>no one</u> has a monopoly on good ideas.

As business owners/managers it is easy to think that we alone know what's best for our business; and with this mindset we can easily trick ourselves into thinking that no one but ourselves can possibly generate ideas which will benefit the business.

How wrong this attitude and perception is!

Unfortunately, as this attitude becomes more and more engrained, people who work in subordinate positions to the owner/manager become disenfranchised from the business – feeling that their ideas/contributions have no worth value. In this scenario, what can typically happen is that employees don't even bother trying to generate creative/new/ innovative ideas, simply leave it to the owner/ manager to "do all the thinking" and do what the owner/manager says verbatim– for they consider that this is how they can stay out of trouble.

The problem with taking this approach is that in the absence of either "new blood" (new people) entering the organization and/or new ideas from existing personnel coming forward, such an organization is prone to stagnating – which generally means it becomes exposed to the very real possibility of losing market share and becoming unviable (please see comments further on in this book regarding the need for businesses to continuously adapt and evolve).

Those organizations that encourage the open and honest exchange of ideas – where no idea is treated as a "bad idea" – tend to be genuinely committed to fostering workplace cultures that are underpinned by desirable principles such as collaboration, cooperation, and inclusivity, and also tend to be the businesses which evolve positively to the greatest extent.

16.0 Surround Yourself With the Best People You Can Afford

As more people in New Zealand make the choice to become tertiary qualified, there is evidence of an interesting trend occurring, whereby despite newly qualified graduates having acquired some of the most up-to-date knowledge in their respective fields, some employers are avoiding employing these people seemingly out of anxiety/fear that the graduate may have a knowledge base which is deeper and/ or broader than their own.

This is an attitude that isn't peculiar to just graduates either. The same avoidance tendency is being seen by some recruitment professionals in respect of well seasoned high achieving experienced people also.

Employers who display this tendency are missing-out on injecting their businesses with considerably talented people, which is at the detriment of their business (see earlier comments re the importance of "new blood" entering organizations to cause them to evolve), and a decision which is causing talented individuals to either transition out of the industry that they were trained to be proficient in and/ or relocate to an alternative region/ country in search of employer mindsets that are more embracing of talented people.

The more commercially mature/savvy business owners/ managers who understand the considerable value a talented person can inject into a business, instead have an attitude of "we'll recruit the best people we can afford". These business owners/managers embrace and nurture talented people – they don't fear them.

Consequently, these businesses tend to flourish, due to having written well defined career paths and by providing ongoing professional development/training opportunities for incoming talented people.

In return for being embraced by their employer, talented people respond by injecting the best of themselves into the business often staying with the business for a long period.

These savvy business owners also understand that if the talented individual proves themselves as a high achieving employee now, then later, the same individual may be a prime candidate to become a company CEO/ GM or shareholder. Which would enable the owner to successively release themselves from their day-to-day involvement in their business – to pursue other interests in life.

In a similar vein, there are some business owners who after engaging a talented employee, become threatened by the employee's growing achievements and/ or their strengthening positive working relationship with (for example) a director or other key personnel; which causes the threatened owner to ultimately manipulate the employee out of the business (e.g. under the guise of a "role disestablishment"). Solicitors in New Zealand are now looking more closely at the justifying reasons for a role becoming disestablished.

If these business owners had taken the time to define a proper career path for the individual, empowering them as much as possible for them to enjoy a high level of autonomy as they pursue their clearly laid-out career path, the outcome could have been very different - and positive - for both parties.

17.0 Controlled Growth Slow and Sure

To minimize the amount of "pain" experienced by your organization, once you have laid the right foundation of Critical Success Factors (see the importance of laying this foundation, as outlined earlier in this book), it is advisable that you grow your trading operation <u>incrementally and in a controlled manner</u>...rather than allow the business to assume its own pace of development.

If your foundation is right to start with, growth will be easier to accommodate and manage as it materializes. In a CEO role that I performed the Company Constitution that was in place had been so carefully formulated that it became subjected to change via shareholder voting processes only twice in the 12 years that I was performing that role.

<u>Plan</u> your growth through your Strategic Plan, and <u>deliver</u> it through your annual Business Plan and annual Marketing Activity Schedule.

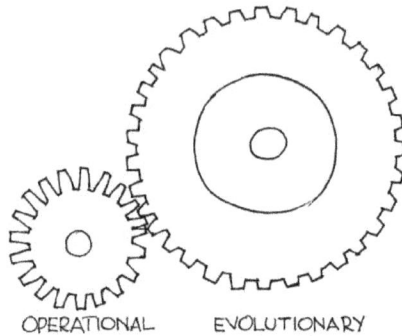

OPERATIONAL   EVOLUTIONARY

18.0 Evolutionary Cogs v Operational Cogs

In mid-large companies in particular, internal stakeholders who are not "at the helm steering the ship" often become frustrated at the lack of forward movement of the company.

Sometimes this perception is actually a close reflection of the reality of the actual situation. I have found that there are a few key reasons for a company slowing- down or stagnating on its evolutionary course:

i)   The owners are so entwined in the day-to-day running of the business, that they have little-no time to work "on" it (i.e. setting direction/exploring new   opportunities for business development/

make timely governance decisions, etc).

ii)   There is no written Strategic Plan in place to evolve the business in any particular direction, or if there is such a plan in place then it either hasn't won the buy-in from internal stakeholders (largely because they haven't been included in its formation) and/ or it hasn't been shared - within the comfort of the owner to disclose particular contents – with relevant stakeholders.

iii) Key internal stakeholders feel disenfranchised from the business.

When I have worked alongside business owners who feel that they've "come unstuck" or are frustrated at feeling like they can't influence any significant momentum in their business, the first question that I ask is "how many days each week are you working on your business and not in it?"

The answers that spring from that initial pivotal question quickly tell me that there is insufficient capacity amongst the owner(s) to work in both the management realm and the governance realm within their business. In short, they are working as "Operational Cogs" in their business – and not as "Evolutionary Cogs".

It is my view that if a business owner is serious/ genuine about wanting to firmly occupy the "governance seat" (become "Evolutionary Cogs") in their business, then they should be doing everything in their power to successively relinquish as many of the day-to-day operational functions that they are involved with as they can – and empower suitably qualified and experienced employees to take care of these instead.

Quality, well reasoned <u>governance</u> decisions made on a timely basis play a huge part in determining the speed at which an organization evolves. The more that "Evolutionary Cogs" are jammed-up dealing with matters which really "Operational Cogs" should be dealing with, the less opportunity there is for such governance decisions to be made...and so the "ship" slows down, and sometimes stops altogether.

19.0 Avoid Paralysis from Analysis

There is a well known saying in the statistics field –
"don't suffer paralysis from too much analysis".

In the Information age that we now live in, we have
sophisticated information systems that allow us to
gain deep insights into all sorts of operating
performance. I have been involved in designing and
developing such systems myself over the years.

Unfortunately, some businesses sometimes fall into
the trap of relying <u>wholly</u> on the data reported by
their information systems to base their commercial
decisions on, involving lengthy and deep analysis. The
danger of doing this is that such data pertains to
events that have <u>already happened </u>(e.g. sales that
have been achieved).

In my opinion, data analysis should be used to understand <u>trends</u> only – to then help decision-makers form predictions around what may or may not happen in the future. Decision-makers need to be careful not to get "bogged down" in infinitesimal data – to the point that no useful decision of any real value is made.

In various management roles that I have performed in I have used data as the main basis for helping me make well considered decisions (for such an empirical approach to management decision-making was instilled in me during my university years), yet have <u>concluded</u> decisions using my experience and intuitive judgment as to what I think the best course of action to take is.

As a director once said to me "it is important to keep one eye on the rear view mirror and one eye looking straight ahead through the front windshield".

On a related topic, I offer a friendly word of caution to business owners and managers, that KPI Performance Reporting can be a double-edged sword if:

i) Too many – or immaterial – performance variables are measured.

ii) Reported data is used irresponsibly to coerce employees to change their behavior/improve their performance.

I have been a part of businesses which have attempted to introduce a myriad of KPI's to measure employee performance against...to their detriment. In response to doing so, what I observed was a dramatic increase in anxiety felt by employees and a reduction in overall productivity and revenue.

Why ? Simple. The more that any individual feels "under the spotlight", and perceives that continuation in their role hinges on them meeting/ exceeding a wide range of targets, the greater the sense of anxiety and futility they will have.

It's no different to including objectives in a Strategic Plan or Business Plan which are wildly unrealistic (e.g. unrealistic timeframe and/ or aspiration). Those people who are expected to realise the plan will quickly interpret the plan as being unobtainable and will be reluctant to apply themselves to the task of setting-out to achieve the given goal.

If people consistently apply their best efforts to achieving a task/ activity, and – according to KPI targets set – consistently fall short of achieving the prescribed targets and consequently are told to "pull their socks-up" each time, most people will become despondent and eventually feel disenfranchised from the business.

This is particularly so where no training resources/ programmes are made available to individuals who are achieving outcomes which are not to the satisfaction of the business owner/ manager.

If you want to bring about positive change in an organization then you must provide the <u>means</u> for the sought after change to be achieved (i.e. through leadership and education/ training).In my view, if you're going to use KPI benchmarking in your business, then limit the number of KPI's that you use to just those that you deem to be essential – and make them <u>few</u> only.

For example:

- Sales $/ unit targets

- Profitability $/ % targets

I have found that providing genuine praise for commendable achievement and encouragement (and guidance) where achievement is waning, works far better from a team culture and morale perspective than a "brick bat" over the head for not meeting a quantitative KPI target.

20.0 Employees/ Contractors: Be Friendly But Not Their Friends

This is an interesting dynamic to explore and understand. In any functional human relationship – and a working relationship between colleagues within an organization is no different – in my opinion we seek to create and foster positive rapport with those who we interact with routinely. In short we try to "get along" with our colleagues.

If we're working with someone day-in and day-out 5 – 7 days a week, the chances are pretty good that we'll become somewhat familiar with at least some aspects of their personal life, over and above their work focus/ experience. Sometimes this familiarity leads to a friendship forming.

As human beings we are all "social animals", and we

generally all strive to belong and be accepted by others. A problem that can inadvertently develop when a business owner or manager befriends an employee who is engaged in a subordinate position is that if/ when it becomes necessary to (constructively) reprimand the employee – or work through a formal disciplinary process with them – it can make it very difficult for the owner/ manager to act objectively and professionally in discharging such responsibilities if a friendship has formed between the employee concerned and the owner/ manager.

A colleague once advised me in relation to the potential for this situation to develop, and wisely suggested that a healthy working relationship between a business owner/ manager and a person who is in a subordinate position to the aforementioned people is where the working relationship is friendly yet not a friendship.

Another important part of the recipe to achieve positive long-term working relationships with employees/ contractors (and not be shocked/ surprised by the sudden departure of particularly your "key players") is to hold a review meeting with each person no less than once every Financial

Year; more than anything to stay <u>attuned to</u> what the employee/ contractor is aspiring to achieve through their working relationship with you/ your business.

Most people have goals of one form or another. If you as a business owner/ manager fail to understand what the goals of particularly the "key players" are in your team, and from their perspective they can't see how the business can help them realise their goals, it is likely that they will look for alternative avenues (e.g. a competitor's business) which they consider have greater potential to help them achieve their goals.

21.0 Start with Local But Don't Forget Global

Thanks largely to the internet and technologies which are compatible with this powerful information network, the world is essentially a global market now; where businesses that are visible in this online space can be connected with by customers located around the world 24 hours/ day, 7 days/ week. Therefore, the opportunity exists for once strongly domestic market orientated businesses to elevate their operations so that their product/ service offer is made available (chiefly via the internet) to customers in other countries. In fact, for those businesses that are looking to expand their market reach and share, such an international expansion strategy could serve them well – and enable them to achieve their growth objectives more quickly than otherwise relying on achieving growth by battling to secure growth in a finite already intensely competitive domestic market. Savvy businesses operating in regions of New Zealand with a strong local/ domestic market focus are increasingly making the realization that the most significant growth in their operation is most likely to come from shifting their focus to increasingly appeal to (and enter) markets in other countries.

Recently I made such a recommendation to a well established vertically structured business. I advocated that they establish strategic partnerships with existing proven retail operations in other countries which are well aligned to their own business (in terms of brand positioning, product offer, business culture, etc) and sell products to these strategic partner retailers on a wholesale basis for these partners to then on-sell these products according to an agreed retail price regime.

I further suggested that a distribution centre per country is all that is needed in order for the New Zealand product provider to have a reliable destination to ship consolidated consignments to – where they can then be sorted into individual store consignments and distributed to their final destination.

Before you start heading-off into the far reaches of the planet, it is advisable that you firstly make sure that your local/ domestic business model is sound and stable, and that you have carefully articulated what your international expansion model looks like in your Strategic Plan and Business Plan.

22.0 Hatching and Nurturing a Positive Work Culture

Many businesses focus the lion's share of their available time, energy, effort and financial resources on achieving their commercial/ financial objectives.

While the necessity to achieve and sustain a viable business is well understood, business owners often overlook the development of their workplace culture as being a major contributing factor to realizing financial success.

In 2015 I was asked by the Chairperson of the Napier Rotary Club (New Zealand) to present to members on any topic of my choosing. I willingly and happily accepted this invitation, and in so doing prepared a PowerPoint presentation to serve as the "backbone" of what I wanted to say about how to evolve an organization.

For those who are interested, this presentation in its entirety can be viewed in my LinkedIn profile found here: https://www.linkedin.com/in/peterdalexander

The essence of this presentation was that, in my opinion and experience, the rate/ speed at which an organization will evolve (become better/ stronger/ larger) very much depends on:

Factor 1: Resource Capacity and Allocation

Plus

Factor 2: People Competencies

Plus

Factor 3: Structure

Plus

Factor 4: Desire/ Will to Change

This relationship can be expressed by the equation:

"e" = Factor 1 + Factor 2 + Factor 3 + Factor 4

...where "e" means the "Speed of Evolution"

And the "oil" which ensures that each of the above Factors are optimized is the <u>culture</u> of the organization.

If you do not have a business environment which is characterised by cultural principles such as "cooperation", "collaboration", "empowerment" and "inclusivity" then your business is more than likely <u>not</u> a happy and (intrinsically) rewarding place for people to work...and unhappy people equates to less-than-optimal productivity and creativity; and can reflect in a relatively high staff turnover rate.

Example of an outstanding positive business culture:

- High level of collaboration

- High level of camaraderie

- Commonly agreed upon decisions are still supported by the opposing minority

- Ready exchange of ideas

Example of an undesirable business culture.

- Poorly communicated stakeholder expectations

- Low level of trust amongst internal stakeholders

- Low level of cooperation and collaboration

Over the years I have observed that the most successful businesses spend time, effort and money on <u>fostering</u> a "great place to work" feeling amongst their team. In such a workplace, people feel:

- Included on the journey.

- Valued.

- They can apply their individual strengths/ characters in their role without fear of being judged

- Naturally drawn to want to help their colleagues.

- That they want to share their honest ideas/ opinions openly.

In my opinion and experience I believe that the extent to which people in positions of authority exert their authority through enforcing legal agreements to try and achieve compliance has a considerable influence on the culture of an organization. As a CEO of a national franchise in New Zealand, the culture of that company was such that I recall only a few instances during my 12 year term in that role when (with Board authorization) I moved to protect the interests of other shareholders by enforcing the provisions of the relevant Shareholder Agreement.

I have found over the years that the least productive way to foster a desirable workplace culture is by threatening a party with the enforcement of a legal agreement. In fact, I regard such a style of management as being immature and compensatory for a lack of people management skills apparent in the person performing the threat.

I have found that it is far more positive and productive to manage the activities and behaviours of other people through managing expectations versus enforcing some legal agreement. Talk with your people...often.

In managing other people who you are leading, set them up to win...equip them with a solid understanding of <u>what you expect them to do</u> (and how) from the outset.

I have three 'Golden Rules" when it comes to managing the activities of other people:

Rule #1:   Never reprimand another person in front of others, and when doing so point out what the individual has been doing that has been <u>right</u> (i.e. in accordance with expectation) – over and above discussing what their unacceptable behavior was that warrants the chat between you and them.

Rule #2:   Be constructive in all feedback/ guidance that is provided to the incumbent. (when warranted) Encourage a positive change of behavior/ attitude in the incumbent – show how this can be achieved.

Rule #3:   Look for opportunities to praise and reward people who are clearly applying themselves to the best of their ability.

I often ponder why it is that as children we receive praise and reward for when we (for example) do a good job of something, help someone else achieve something of merit, etc...yet when we become adults such praise and reward is seldom seen or heard?

Having coached kids in junior sport I have seen the positive difference it makes for a child to be told they "kicked a great goal" or they "had a superb game"; compared to other coaches who snarl at and criticize players for not achieving what the coach thinks they're capable of achieving.

As a leader (business owner/ manager) it is important to remember that each individual has their own strengths/ weaknesses and a unique ability to perform. In my view, what matters most is that people strive to be the best they can be at what they do...and the people who are responsible for encouraging performance duly recognize and reward individuals when they consider that the individual is in fact applying themselves to the best of their ability.

I use a simple "barometer" to gauge the positive strength of a workplace culture. I consider that a First Class workplace culture is evident when I can see colleagues helping one-another <u>without</u> having being asked to do so by the person who they report to.

It is surprising to see the number of businesses where employees still operate in "silo" situations. This is where an employee operates virtually in isolation of their colleagues – concentrating exhaustively on performing the work scope that is reflected in the Job Description; and has no predisposition to work collaboratively. I have seen this culture in organizations that pride themselves on having a "flat structure" as well as in relation to vertically structured organizations.

I have found that workplaces which encourage "silo" situations are generally not happy workplaces to work in, and the businesses concerned generally don't evolve at the same rate as those which encourage a more collaborative, cooperative and inclusive dynamic to exist between internal stakeholders.

Another major contributing reason as to why organizations fail to evolve at a commendable rate is that the people who are in positions of authority attempt to <u>control</u> the people who they are appointed to manage the activities of.

It is absolutely detrimental to human relationships (in all aspects of human life) for one person to try and control the thoughts and actions of another person. Such controlling behavior will only result in frustration and resentment...and if it perseveres, the breakdown of a functional relationship.

Overbearing control can most certainly cause people to feel suppressed, oppressed, and hamstrung. Often fear develops in the subordinate, causing them to be distracted from doing a good job by the fear that has been instilled in them. Control is <u>counter-productive</u> to people becoming the best that they can be – it strips people of their sense of individuality, and dampens enthusiasm, creativity, flair, innovation and imagination - and will often cause people not to contribute ideas towards the advancement of the given organisation.

From what I have experienced as a senior manager to date, I rate induced anxiety/fear as the #1 reason why organizations don't progress/evolve to realise their potential. Fear is a "handbrake" that will stifle the forward movement of any organization.

"Controlling" other people is not an effective management style/practice. Rather, it is more about a demonstration of power.

The opposite can be said about <u>empowerment</u>. If you want to bring the best out of any person – for them to win at their pursuit, in my opinion there is no more powerful way of achieving this than by empowering the individual with as much discretion and autonomy to decide and act as you can (still with you guiding them <u>if/when</u> they ask for it).

As a result of doing so you may well see the empowered individual:

- Show more pride and dedication towards their pursuit.

- Achieve a higher quality and/ or greater result.

- Want to pursue more/ other/ new tasks/ activities.

- Want to take on greater responsibility.

- Display greater trust and respect towards you.

My final "words of wisdom" that I'd like to offer on the topic of building a desirable workplace culture is that as a leader (business owner/ manager) encourage genuine views/ contributions to come forward from your team.

I have seen some businesses slow down due to the owners being somewhat dictatorial in their management style – to the extent that the stakeholders who reported to them became anxious about stating their honest opinions to them for fear of reprisal.

If something doesn't work – for whatever reason, then it is in the best interests of the organization (as a whole) for the person in the relevant position of authority to be told that this is the case; so the issue can be resolved and the organization can move forward.

23.0 Capturing Lost Opportunities

A great way of refining and improving your customer value proposition is to practice the discipline of recording "Lost Opportunities".

A "Lost Opportunity" occurs when a customer – after all persuasive influence provided by marketing stimulus/ sales people – still doesn't commit to purchase a product/ service that they took an interest in.

A "Lost Opportunity" represents a future opportunity for a business to make a successful sale...if the "Lost Opportunity" is recorded soon after it occurs and is communicated to the relevant person within the business for them to effect action to have the perceived gap filled.

I have seen the capture and communication of "Lost Opportunities" produce considerable positive effects. This practice has allowed the businesses concerned to either modify some design element of an existing product and/ or introduce a brand new product to fill the perceived gap in their respective product mix.

The key is for the client to be politely asked "why" they chose not to proceed with making a purchase, at the point they are ready to disengage with the business. This can easily be achieved in-store by skilled sales people – discretely incorporating the question in their farewell to the customer.

24.0 Monitor, Measure, Review

In order to make good well informed decisions which help a business to evolve, it is important to capture and use pertinent information.

Many businesses are increasing the level of insight into their operations by installing sophisticated Business Intelligence Systems – which use the raw data from their everyday transactions to report outcomes such as:

- Profitability per product category

- Sales performance per product category

- Sell-through rate per product category

A proven great practice to employ is to use whatever information system your business operates with to monitor, measure and review operational performance in relation to key indices (such as the parameters above). Again, avoid getting "bogged down" in infinitesimal data and look for the trends (only).

Use this three-staged process to test new initiatives (e.g. a new product offer). Implement the initiative, then monitor, measure and review the commercial effect it had in the market. Allow the review determinations to influence you to adjust/ withdraw/ replace the initiative, and once again monitor, measure and review its market impact.

Helpful Hint –

One reliable and proven way of measuring the effect of a retail marketing campaign is to have an "electronic people counter" installed per entrance into your store.

These counters typically use infrared technology. An infrared beam is cut (interfered with) each time a customer enters (and departs) which causes a count figure to register.

Over a period of time the business owner can see what the "average number of visitors" is per day/ week/ month/ year. Then when a marketing promotion is implemented it becomes possible to compare the visitor numbers which eventuated during the promotion timeframe with the "average number of visitors" received in the absence of such a promotion. Such a comparison helps the business owner determine to what extent the given promotion has been successful at influencing people to visit...and therefore help the business owner to decide whether there is merit in repeating the same or similar promotion – and if so, during what timeframe next time.

It is possible to calculate a Sales Conversion Rate using the figure taken from an electronic people counter, as follows:

- Firstly divide the total raw count figure (e.g. 1200) for whatever timeframe by a devisor/ factor which recognizes that this figure includes both those instances when a customer entered the store and when they exited...plus to recognize that sometimes a visitor is accompanied by a child (in a pram or otherwise). Over the years I have advocated that "2.5" be used as the divisor.

So in the above example 1200 divided by 2.5 = 480 (which is the approximate number of customers that visited during the timeframe being reviewed).

- Next divide the total number of product units that were purchased during the period under review by the number of customers who visited during this same period, to calculate the Sales Conversion Rate.

- Using the above example again, if the total number of product units purchased by customers was 350, and the total number of customers who visited the store during the review under review was 480, then the Sales Conversion rate = 350/ 480 = 73 % (if it is considered that on average 1 x product unit is purchased per customer per customer visit occasion.

- The Sales Conversion Rate is one of the most important KPI's that particularly a bricks and mortar based business can measure and monitor; for it provides a quick understanding of how effective the sales team is being at converting "browsers" into "buyers".

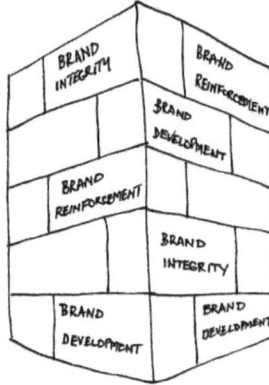

25.0 Brand Development, Reinforcement and Integrity

It is surprising to still see relatively little attention being paid by some business owners to developing/ achieving a business brand which:

➢ Is distinctly unique in its design
➢ Is simplistic in its construct – and comprises only a small number of elements and range of colour
➢ Is easy for a viewer to distinguish what it is
➢ Is easy for a viewer to associate it with the nature of business that it represents
➢ Is memorable

> Stands-out...has market cut-through amongst other brands

> Is easily scalable (while retaining legibility) and can be applied to a wide range of usage situations (e.g. QR Codes, banners, car signage, print advertising, etc)

Many business still choose to use their legal name as their trading identity/ business brand.

What is also concerning is that in a large number of cases that I have seen while performing as a Business Advisor in the Hawke's Bay region (New Zealand) where a distinct business brand has been developed, the business owner hasn't then taken the prudent step of having it registered as a Trade Mark with the Intellectual Property Office of New Zealand (please see the importance of registering a brand as intellectual property, as stated earlier in this book).

Having developed a brand, what is **"Brand Reinforcement"** then?

It is the degree to which a business promotes its brand and business proposition in the market using marketing stimulus that is <u>aligned</u>. A poor brand reinforcement strategy would be where ½ dozen different depictions of a brand logo are used across say 3 – 4 different consecutive ads. Whereas a good brand reinforcement strategy is where a company uses the <u>same</u> basic "shell" (template) for communicating its marketing message.

General Rule of Thumb:

Generally, the greater the <u>uniformity</u> achieved in how a brand and business is marketed, the more firmly the brand and business will be reinforced in consumer minds...which will cause greater **awareness** of that brand/ business to occur more quickly.

That's how our memories and recall work. The more often we see/ taste/ hear/ feel/ smell something, the more that experience becomes cemented in our mind...and the more readily we are able to recall it.

What is "**Brand Integrity**" then?

Every <u>positive</u> experience that a customer associates with a brand serves to <u>build</u> the integrity/ positive reputation of that brand and business. Example behaviours that can positively impact a brand include: how we conduct ourselves when meeting with clients, the speed at which we turn around replies to client queries... and the clarity of our answers.

Conversely, every <u>negative</u> experience that a

customer associates with a brand serves to <u>reduce</u> the integrity/ reputation of that brand and business.

Because brand integrity is <u>integrally</u> related to how customers perceive us/ our business, everything we say and do will either build or reduce our (business) brand integrity. It is just as easy to lose brand integrity as it is to gain it. It takes a <u>lot</u> of energy and commitment (attitudinal/ financial/ behavioural) to build and maintain brand awareness and integrity.

General Rule of Thumb:

Generally, those businesses that enjoy a high level of brand integrity also enjoy <u>high customer brand awareness ratings and a considerable share of their respective markets</u>.

26.0 The Most Deep-rooted Relationships Are Those That Are Formed Face-to-Face

As digital technology enables more and more electronic means by which people can connect with one another, it is important to remember that there is a significant segment of the population aged mid 40's and older who have grown- up in environments (home/school/workplace) which have encouraged the <u>spoken</u> language – and where everyday <u>face-to-face</u> interaction was commonplace.

This demographic prides itself on its ability to hold open, honest and sometimes drawn-out verbal conversations...conversations which engender a strong sense of trust and rapport between those talking...conversations which cannot come close to being replicated in terms of quality, emotional exchange and depth of connection by "Liking" someone's Facebook page or by connecting with them through some other digital platform.

As electronic communications become favoured by a greater population of people, there is already evidence of considerable value being placed on face-to- face interaction - with more people joining clubs and finding social avenues to be able to connect face-to-face with others.

And therein lies a considerable opportunity for bricks and mortar businesses that are prepared to provide first class customer service. I believe that the strongest positive connections that people make are those that are face-to-face; providing that the conversation is not contrived, the language and subject matter doesn't offend, and what is being spoken about has value/ benefit for the parties who are engaged in conversation.

I strongly suggest that business owners/ managers should be teaching particularly younger employees the art of holding a good old fashion verbal conversation with customers. Conversation which is genuine, free-flowing and which provides some value (e.g. insight) to both parties. Particularly in the case of Kiwis, New Zealand customers typically feel a little annoyed being engaged by store personnel who obviously are singularly focused on clinching a sale.

The more savvy businesses are teaching their sales teams how to engage in conversation after meeting/greeting people that enter their stores...and guide the customer only if/when the customer becomes ready to be helped.

The key is to allow customers maximum choice, and only help to the extent that they wish to be helped...always providing genuine advice/feedback/input when they ask for help/guidance.

The more that customers feel that salespeople have truly wanted to engage with them in an open and genuine manner in order to get to know them generally at least a little, the stronger the "bridge of trust" and regard/respect will exist between the salesperson and the customer.

27.0 Identifying, Measuring and Assessing Risk

Identifying, measuring and taking risk is a part of everyday human life. It is also an inherent part of being a business owner and decision-makers (e.g. CEO/ GM) who have the responsibility of making prudent decisions in the best interests of the organisations that they represent.

Sadly, I have seen a steady decline in New Zealand generally in the ability and willingness of particularly younger people who are appointed to senior management (i.e. leadership) positions to make timely and well-informed quality decisions. I consider that part of the reason for this is due to our tendency as a nation to "wrap our children in cotton wool" – to protect them from the perceived evils of the world.

Unfortunately, by insulating our children in this way, it has prevented them from having to "stand on their own two feet" and assess new situations, identify any apparent risks involved and make decisions as to what action they deem appropriate to take having weighed-up the various risks involved.

I have seen even very large companies that are fortunate to have highly skilled/ experienced personnel in key functions perform analysis after analysis in relation to a new initiative that it wants to implement...and procrastinate the "go ahead or not" decision for an unnecessarily protracted timeframe, even though the analysis performed clearly revealed the right decision to be that of "go ahead".

Equally unfortunately, it seems that the general mindset prevalent in New Zealand (and other countries) now is that of a "risk averse" person. As "risk minimization" continues to take hold in New Zealand (and other parts of the world) it could be argued that profit realization will generally diminish proportionately. For (as my age group were taught at the young age of 13 years) profit is the reward for taking a risk, and if businesses are increasingly not prepared to take risks (and/ or are prevented from being allowed to take reasonable risks) then the profit realized by businesses generally can be expected to diminish in my view.

28.0 Challenge the Status Quo of Your Business

Particularly at the time of reviewing and re-setting your Strategic Plan, don't be afraid to <u>challenge</u> the current modus operandi (i.e. the operational status quo) of your business.

Be honest with yourself as to what aspects of the business are working well...versus those that are not. A well known truism which has been a part of human evolution for centuries is that if we do nothing more or nothing different to what we have practiced to date, the best we can expect is the continuation of outcomes/ results as have historically transpired.

Particularly at the time of reviewing and re-setting your Strategic Plan, don't be afraid to <u>challenge</u> the current modus operandi (i.e. the operational status quo) of your business.

To varying extents we are all "creatures of habit"…we find comfort in doing things which are familiar to us. Unfortunately engrained habits are dangerous for people, because they cause us to act somewhat automatically/mindlessly and they undermine the opportunity for us to think innovatively/creatively to push boundaries to discover new fertile ground on which to develop new interests.

The extent to which we are prepared to accommodate/ embrace change has a defining influence on our lives – business and personal alike. I believe that the willingness of business owners to:

- Challenge the modus operandi of their own business – to streamline/ fine-tune it.

- Allow others (either within and/ or outside their business) to objectively assess their business (e.g. through a GAP Analysis or similar) to understand where the opportunities exist for improving the operation.

- Overall want to change themselves/some

aspect of their operation....

is <u>hugely</u> influential in how – and the extent to which – the given business evolves and realizes success.

Charles Darwin was perceptive in determining the following...

> "It is not the strongest of the species that survives, nor the most intelligent that survives. It is the one that is most **adaptable to change**"

It was interesting talking with the Rector of a highly regarded Hawke's Bay secondary school during 2016, who had attended an international conference of Principals from around the world. This Rector conveyed to me that a key message communicated at this conference was how important it has become for students around the world to learn the skill of being <u>adaptable</u> as they edge closer towards entering the workforce (and then continue to develop their adaptability having become a part of the workforce).

When you make the determination to change some aspect/ dimension of your business, <u>commit</u> that decision to your Strategic Plan...and subsequently your annual Business Plan. By doing so you will improve your chances of implementing the changes that you have deemed necessary to make.

Remember – change is just that...change. The key to implementing change which positively impacts an organization is:

a) Tell the people who will be affected by the change <u>before</u> implementation commences. Learn what their fears/concerns are – and address/ resolve these.

b) Show the people who will be affected by the change what the implications of the pending change are.

c) Keep updating affected people as to progress being made implementing the given change, throughout the implementation timeframe.

29.0 Building a United Governance Body

It is not uncommon for directors (particularly where a Board consists of multiple directors...say 4 or more directors) to hold opposing views on issues/ topics/ opportunities – sometimes to the extent that an impasse occurs.

In addition, directors on the same given Board have been known to not visibly support decisions made by at least the majority of directors, when a Board resolution is communicated wider afield to shareholders. Such conflicting behaviour can serve to instil a sense of low confidence and/ or unrest amongst shareholders, who (in their minds) see a Board which can't agree – and therefore can't act in a united way to serve the best interests of shareholders and the greater company.

For most particularly shareholders to feel confident in their elected Board, it is critical that directors demonstrate a <u>united front</u> when communicating governance decisions to stakeholders. In practice this means that the minority of directors who were defeated in relation to a particular Board resolution, still visibly show their support of the governance decision that was made – despite not backing it at the time the decision was made.

Companies – particularly larger companies – that are committed to practicing good governance often choose to develop and work in accordance with a **'Board Code of Conduct'**. Although the scope and content of such a document can/ will differ from company to company, the primary purpose of a Board Code of Conduct is to define and clarify:

a) The scope of Director authority in respect of company decision-making, and particularly in relation to financial decisions that impact on all shareholders.

b) The way in which Directors approach, resolve, and implement Board decisions – and the standards of behaviour and interaction that are expected within the Board forum.

c) The dynamics and functionality which must exist between appointed Directors in order to remain a united and progressive decision-making body; and in order to be seen and respected as such by shareholders.

In respect of the Codes of Conduct that I have been involved in preparing, the following topics/ focuses have been deemed as key inclusions by the Boards concerned:

- Scope of Board decision-making in respect of financial decisions

- Governance style – e.g. All Directors must be committed to managing the business affairs of the company in a manner that achieves governance decisions being made on a timely basis, that are in the best interests of at least the majority of shareholders on each occasion, and which contribute towards advancing the company as a whole towards its identified strategic objectives.

- Discussion and decision input – e.g. provide direct and timely input into governance issues which Directors are responsible for resolving, irrespective of whether the request for input occurs within or outside of a formal Board meeting – and always by any specified time deadline.

- Fair opportunity to express genuine views – e.g. Board meetings are provided to allow a fair exchange of genuine views amongst Directors. It is the Board Chairperson's responsibility to ensure that no one Director dominates discussion, and each Director must display the courtesy of allowing fellow Directors to express their views.

- Shareholder best interests – e.g. Directors are committed to making decisions that will benefit most shareholders most of the time. Whilst outlying individual attitudes and/ or views of certain shareholders may be taken into account during Board discussion on a particular issue, the final Board decision made will reflect benefiting the majority of shareholders each time.

- Universal support of Board resolutions

formed –

e.g. When a Board resolution has been formed and committed to recorded Board minutes - irrespective of the nature, content, or ramifications/ implications of the resolution – each and every Director will support that decision to all shareholders.

- Delegation of authority to act – e.g. The Board may choose to empower either an appropriate Director and/ or employee of the company to act on its behalf – including make decisions and take action within a prescribed work scope set by the Board.

- Board consultation with shareholders – e.g. At any time, the Board is free to choose to consult with one or more shareholder of the company to either receive input contributions into governance decisions and/ or discuss issues which the Board is required to make decisions in relation to.

- Notice required in relation to director absenteeism.

- Assignment of projects to directors – e.g. One

or more director may be assigned project work for delivery from time to time. All such projects must be scoped definitively, sized, have a monetary value put against them, and approved by way of a Board resolution.

- Director attendance at Board meetings – e.g. Unless adverse or unforeseen situations – or planned leave from the business - mean that a Director cannot attend a scheduled Board meeting, all Directors are otherwise expected to attend each scheduled meeting – particularly face-to-face Board meetings.

By having a Board Code of Conduct in place, governance processes (including decision-making) should flow better, with less conflict occurring during Board meetings. Overall, such a document should help the given company achieve less procrastination and greater momentum.

30.0 Online Availability of this Book

This book is available for sale via the Amazon book store at https://www.amazon.com/

Search author's name or Rangitawa Publishing

It is also possible to access this book online via these websites:

www.realworldconsulting.kiwi

www.rangitawapublishing.com

If you are interested to read about Peter's background, he has a LinkedIn profile located here: https://www.linkedin.com/in/peterdalexander

Acknowledgements

A big thank you to Jill at Rangitawa Publishing and illustrators Gael and Allen Gamble who transformed my writing into a well presented and appealing book. You can find out more about Rangitawa Publishing here: www.rangitawapublishing.com

I am also enormously grateful to my brother – Matthew Alexander – for his creative input into the design of the Real World Consulting business logo and his talents in producing various marketing IP which supports Real World Consulting Limited in the global market...not least of which is the Real World Consulting website. Matt is an accomplished graphic designer, web designer and multi-media specialist (to name just a few of his talents). You can find out more about Matt here:

https://linkedin.com/in/mralexandernz

I am also very thankful to the various people who saw merit in appointing me to the management roles which I have worked in over the years. It is these opportunities/role appointments which have allowed me to gain the experience, insight and knowledge that has served as the inspiration and basis for this book.

My hope is that somehow and in some way this book will help particularly those people who have helped me along the way, to shape and sustain more successful and rewarding businesses.

I leave you with these parting words...

My belief is that the greatest sense of fulfilment that a business owner or senior manager can hope to feel is when the business that they are responsible for leading achieves a workplace culture which is at least as favourable as their financial/commercial achievements.

www.ingramcontent.com/pod-product-compliance
Lightning Source LLC
Chambersburg PA
CBHW071552200326
41519CB00021BB/6708